Further Adventures of Tabitha Miggins, Ship's Cat on the Pill Ferry

A Modern Day Ferry Tale

Other Bristol-related books available from Bristol Folk Publications

Tabitha Miggins, Ship's Cat (on the Pill Ferry) *(the first book in the series)*

Bristol Folk: a Discographical History of Bristol Folk Music in the 1960s and 1970s *(Illustrated; includes reminiscences from those that were there, including Fred Wedlock and internationally-renowned fantasy artist, Rodney Matthews, who started out designing posters for Bristol's folkies)*

The Saydisc and Village Thing Discography *(Illustrated; these record labels were responsible for some of the finest Bristolian [and non-Bristolian] music ever released)*

Further Adventures of Tabitha Miggins, Ship's Cat on the Pill Ferry

A Modern Day Ferry Tale

Mark Clinton Jones

BRISTOL FOLK PUBLICATIONS
BRISTOL ● BRINDLE HOLM ● THE SNUG

Further Adventures of Tabitha Miggins, Ship's Cat on the Pill Ferry
published 2015 by Bristol Folk Publications www.bristol–folk.co.uk

Paperback edition: ISBN 978-1-909953-65-9

Copyright © Mark Clinton Jones 2015. Cover illustration copyright © J. D. Bird 2015.

The right of Mark Clinton Jones to be identified as the Author of this work and the right of J. D. Bird to be identified as the illustrator of this work have been asserted in accordance with the Copyrights, Designs and Patents Act 1988.

All rights reserved. No part of this book may be reprinted or reproduced or utilised or transmitted in any form or by any means, electronic or mechanical, including photocopy, recording, or any information storage and retrieval system, including the Internet, now known or hereafter invented, without permission in writing from the copyright holder.

Layout, design and digital/physical realisation by Bristol Folk Publications.

Further Adventures of Tabitha Miggins...

Contents

1. Carry on Miggins 3
2. From home to home 21
3. Up the creek without a waddle 28
4. May Day, mayhem and Morris Men 46
5. Tabitha Miggins changes the course of history (by accident) 53
6. Pill, Pill, ich liebe dich noch 84
7. Tabitha Miggins changes the course of history (by design) 94
8. Last orders for Tabitha Miggins 105
9. Epilogue 127
10. Coda 131
About the author 132
What others are saying about Miggins 134

In memory of *Kevyn Rhys Jones* (24th May 1953 to 21st February 2015), who provided the joke about the tank before pottering off far too early, and to our elderly, knitting-mad, slightly tipsy, tabby cat, *Mother* (somewhere between 1993 and 1997, depending on which vet you believe, to 27 May 2015).

Thanks to Neil at my ex-local for a spontaneous 'nein down' at just the right moment and to *The Salutation* at Ham for brewing extremely potable (if not downright magical) beer. Is it merely coincidence, I wonder, that it is slap-bang next door to another Ham Green and just a few hundred yards from another Pill? Good heavens, Milk Stout on as well, last visit! I think that Miggins would approve.

Further Adventures of Tabitha Miggins...

1. Carry on Miggins

Well, hello, Dear Hearts, so nice to see you again – and what do you know! They've let me put together another collection of reminiscences, based on the surprisingly large number of sales of my first literary outing. Who'd have thought that it would have proven so popular? I mean, sales are evidently now in double figures. It even sold a few copies across The River, which I'll never live down.

    I was very upset, however, by some very unkind words from one particular critic, who said something along the lines of the last book being completely devoid of plot. What rubbish! There were lots of plots, it's just that I could never quite remember which one I was supposed to be telling you about at any given time. This, perhaps, because I spend so much time gallivanting about *in* time. And add to this my various lives – and deaths, of course – and it all gets very complicated. So is it any wonder that I get confused?

    "Linear time is a luxury. Well, for some of us, at least."

    That's what I said to Captain Bastable at the *Time Centre* a few weeks ago, as we enjoyed a chinwag over a Milk Stout or two. Nice chap, old Oswald, providing that you keep him off the subject of airships and atom bombs. He's got a bit of a thing about them, if you ask me – and what Clement Freud would make of that is anyone's guess. Well, be that as it may, I'll have to tell you about Oswald and my other friends up at the *Centre* one of these days. Another thing about time is that the more of it you put behind you, the faster it seems to go. And, of course, life itself has its ups and downs, if you'll pardon my resorting to the funicular.

    I'm so sorry, I've started to ramble a bit earlier than usual, haven't I, Dear Hearts? Where was I? Oh yes, introducing this current tome – but, before I forget, there was another, quite odd, review that said something along the lines of, "This is not quite a children's book, but is one that should be enjoyed by those with a bit of child in their makeup," which made me wonder if I wasn't writing for ogres.

    Anyway, an awful lot has happened since I last put paw to paper and added to that is the fact that so many of my friends from down the years have got in touch to remind me of a whole host of things that escaped my memory the first time around. I probably have more than enough to fill a whole book with reminiscences involving Lavinia, though I feel that she would prefer me to keep much of her dead past hid. There's probably enough amongst the correspondence to have her sectioned at the least, if not banged up in the slammer for a good, long time.

What's that, Dear Hearts? Won't I tell at least one of the stories about Lavinia? Well, alright, but just one. But which one? I mean, there are just so many. Oh, I know, what about the time she disappeared from the Consulate in Ankara? She turned up eventually, having been tracked down to some Pasha's harem. She was an obelisk there, or something, unlikely as that sounds. How she got involved with the Pasha in the first place never was fully explained, though I remember her telling me that she got off to a bad start when she made herself comfortable on his personal chaise longue. Evidently, it was not intended for infidels, such as Lavinia, but was solely for the Ottoman to put his bottom on.

She had been forced to learn some fairly specialised dancing in the harem and thought that she could make use of her newfound skills once back in this country, so she put together a rather risqué act for working men's clubs and such like. After all, she was on long-term sick leave from The Service for her nerves following the certain amount of touch-and-go diplomacy that had been needed to extricate her from the harem, so she had to find something to do with her time.

So as to give her act a bit of local colour when she was over this side of the country she billed it as 'The Dance of the Severn Vale'. She also used to do a variation for elderly gents in some of the more progressive nursing homes that she called 'The Dance of the Seven Filing Cabinets'. It was pretty much the same, except that during the act she had rather more sets of drawers to divest, so as to keep the elderly audience's interest up, though in practice most had generally nodded off into their cocoa long before it got too exciting.

Well, I'd better move away from Lavinia and tell you about this current set of ruminations or the whole book will be taken up with her misadventures. So we'll be hearing about a few old friends as well as about one fearsome enemy – and there are one or two new faces around as well. Of course, there have been quite a few exciting adventures – and a fair few banal ones too, come to that. What you really want to hear about, though I have to admit that I find bits of it quite embarrassing, is the time that I altered the entire course of history and helped the Germans to win World War Two. And it was all because when I went into the future to have a little chat with myself I forgot to explain things fully.

History got better, of course, as it always does, but it was a close run thing and, although I say it myself, it was my good self that saved the day – still, I think we'll sidle up to that particular story after I'd told you about a few other things that have happened in the meantime. But where to start, Dear Hearts? That's always the problem with writing.

Well, my mind's suddenly a blank. Could this be writer's block, I wonder. Perhaps I should just limber up a bit with...oh dear, but with what?

Oh, I know; forget everything I said just now about not telling you more about Lavinia quite yet. I might as well start this particular tome by telling you just a few more things – I'm sure she won't mind. Well, to be honest, when the book is published I'll just tear out the first chapter from her copy; she'll never notice. And, besides, anything to delay telling you about my slight temporal and historical faux pas.

Besides, Lavinia's at the top of my mind at the moment because it was only a few nights ago that she told me about her latest business idea – she's having about three ideas a week now that she's stuck up at *The Home* with nothing but endless jigsaws to do, what with having given up knitting now that her joints are starting to play up a bit. Anyway, this one is probably less ludicrous than the last thirty or so, though that's not saying much. She's evidently been running with this one for a while, but has only just let on about it.

What's that, Dear Hearts? What is this business idea? Well, I'm coming to it by degrees, don't you know? Don't distract me or you'll break my train of thought. Now, where was I?

Oh, yes, Lavinia's latest idea. Well, would you believe that she wants to start up as a Designer Dream Consultant? She's been experimenting with different combinations of cheese to see if there are discernible effects on resultant dreams and thinks that she will soon have a workable set of results for which the rich and stupid will pay good dinero.

"Tell me what you want to dream about," she said to me, "And I'll advise, for a hefty fee, obviously, which combination of cheeses you need to eat just before bedtime so as to attain those dreams."

I asked her, for want of anything else to say, really – and after a lengthy pause, whilst I let it all sink in – if there were any combinations to avoid and she suggested not to eat 30g of vindaloo Limburger along with 15g of harissa-infused Wensleydale and 10g of jalapeno Cheshire just before bed.

"Why?" I asked, "Does it give you terrible nightmares of some description."

"No," she replied, "It just gives you terrible indigestion, followed by near-terminal wind."

Well, this probably explains why she now has such a remote room up at *The Home*. In fact, I'd already heard from Rat-a-Tat and Sticky Paws that, for weeks, Lavinia's fearful screams and other odd noises during the night had kept everyone else awake, hence her removal to an old, disused wing where she can howl to her heart's content. I'm beginning to wonder whether there are any cheese combinations that give you pleasant dreams.

Oh, good heavens, Dear Hearts, I'd almost forgotten one embarrassment involving Lavinia back in the days when our brave lads were still out in Afghanistan. A nice, young squaddie, home on leave, was chatting to some of his contemporaries at the snug at *The Duke* one evening, when Lavinia, who had popped along for a sweet sherry before heading back to *The Home* for her pre-bedtime jigsaw, overheard him say that he had just returned from a tour of Helmand.

"Oh, how wonderful that must have been," she'd chirruped in that gushing way of hers, "I'd love to see how they make their mayonnaise! Who do you have to see to go on the tour?"

He was very polite I thought, but we heard him and his chums laughing fit to bust as they headed down to *The Star* a few minutes later. Lavinia, of course, was oblivious and seemed well pleased with the piece of paper on which the squaddie had jotted down the phone number of the local Army Recruitment Agency. I wonder what she thought when she got back to *The Home* and put on her glasses? I hope that she didn't just phone the number; after all, she's daft enough to get enlisted, especially now she looks so kittenish again, and goodness knows where she'd end up then.

Still, that was comparatively recently, but it's the old memories that have so much more currency. I remember walking around Soho with her, window shopping in those impecunious days. Well, an insalubrious Tom came up as we were wandering down a side alley somewhere near Frith

Street and asked us if we had the time. I was just getting out my sturdy fob watch and was scandalised when Lavinia chimed in with, "Yes, if you've got the dinero!"

I also remember when we were revising for our EO exams just before The War – we were both in the Air Ministry at this point. Anyway, Lavinia, always a bundle of nerves at the best of times, used to turn into a quivering, tearful jelly if you so much as mentioned the word 'exam'. Revision never really sat well with her – after all, it's so boring, isn't it? – and on the few occasions that she could be bothered to read something it just failed to go in so, credulous to the core, she went out and bought a special, lucky crystal, which was said to aid memory. Actually sitting down and making some proper revision notes might have been better for her, but she'd do anything to avoid the job in hand.

Anyway, I can readily recall the to-do twenty minutes into the exam when she remembered that she'd forgotten to bring the lucky crystal with her. We all got an extra ten minutes for that particular one, whilst Lavinia was led off for a lie down in a darkened room with a cologne-soaked silk handkerchief on her brow. I don't know if she ever did retake the exam, but I was later told that, thanks to some well-placed hysterics in front of The Board, she'd ended up being given an ægrotat. I'm not quite sure to this day what one of those is, Dear Hearts, but I have a vague idea that it's a wading bird of some kind. A funny thing to give her, I always thought. I wonder what happened to it.

Whilst I think of it, what with having just mentioned The War, I ended up at *Bletchley Park* cracking codes and all that malarkey, don't you know, Dear Hearts – and all thanks to Lavinia, of course. Here's how it all happened. One day a memo was sent around the Air Ministry asking if there was anyone in the department that spoke German and was good at cryptic crosswords. As you know, Dear Hearts, if you've been attentive – or, at least, if you've read my first book – I spoke German like a native in those days, though it's a bit rusty from disuse now, and I was also jolly good at getting the better of old Torquemada in an hour or so each morning.

I'll tell you, though, that I had the fantods good and proper over that memo. It didn't say why they wanted to know and I had visions, if admitting my skills, of being trained up as spy and being dropped behind the German lines. Well, I was determined not to respond to that particular memo if I could help it and just keep well and truly schtum. Of course, I'd forgotten Lavinia's ability to be helpful at just the wrong times.

First thing the next morning the Head of the Department was wandering from office to office with various important-looking people in civvies asking the question again – and the fact that yesterday's memo was being followed up like this told us all that there must be something at the back of it all. I could never tell an untruth – that's not my way – but I could just stay silent when asked with a look on my face that could be taken for 'Sadly, no.'

Well, the question was asked and I did an excellent impersonation of someone who neither spoke German nor who had just hidden the latest half-completed Torquemada under a pile of requisitions.

At which point Lavinia, who'd just appeared in the room, bag of buns in hand, chirruped in with, "Oh, Tabitha speaks awfully good German – won prizes at Kittengarten for it, she did."

Attention passed Migginswards and the head asked me again if I spoke German. Despite my innate inability to lie, I suddenly saw myself stood against a wall refusing a blindfold and denial came almost unbidden. Unfortunately, what with being put on the spot, my denial came in German of all things! Well, it was topmost on my mind in the circs.

"Nein!" I said, complete with comedy German accent, reddening somewhat under my tabby exterior as I realised what I'd just said.

Well, at least I hadn't given away that I knew anything about crosswords. Perhaps one out of two wouldn't be good enough to qualify for being shot.

Meanwhile, one of the officials in civvies spoke.

"Nein?" he asked, with a querulous eyebrow raised.

"Oh," said Lavinia, still clueless, "She must mean nine down – she was having a bit of a problem with that one just before I headed out to buy the buns. You know, old Torquemada in *The Observer* – she's a fiend when it comes to cryptic crosswords."

Talk about fast work. I arrived at *Bletchley Park* about two and a half hours later, quaking in my boots until they told me what it was all about. And jolly interesting it all turned out to be.

Anyway, Lavinia saw out The War in the jolly, old Air Ministry, where I briefly rejoined her once hostilities were over. However, I soon ended up in post-war Germany with the Control Commission, what with 'German speaker' – not to mention 'Bad liar' – being written in very big letters on my records. Funny, what with all these twists and turns in my career, that both Lavinia and myself should end up as Colonial Companions a few years later.

Well, we saw much less of each other for some years because we were generally posted to very different parts of the world and, as I mentioned in the last book, Lavinia was always very quickly posted on following some indiscretion or other, that or because of some overt display of devastatingly bad judgement. Still, we always kept in touch, mostly by post back in those halcyon days when you could pop a letter into the box at Kabul one day and have it arrive promptly in the Bahamas only six months later. What with Lavinia being posted on so often, some of my letters to her took years to catch up.

Of her letters to myself, I remember one particular letter from her in which she told me all about her first encounter with a possum. She was working next door to the Australian equivalent of *Somerset House* and used to see the possum wandering in every morning and leaving every afternoon and had assumed that he worked there. Well, she'd bumped into him in the street one day and asked if he was a fellow Civil Servant, to which he said that he wasn't. So she'd asked him why he spent so much time at the records office, to which he'd answered that he was a genealogist. Well, of course, Lavinia had never heard of the word, so he explained further that he spent most of his time looking up his family tree. Lavinia's rather baffled reply was exquisite in the extreme.

"Why?" she'd said, "Do you keep falling out?"

Later on, of course, telephones became a lot more widespread and reliable, so we also managed to get to hear various bits of news from each other whilst it was still fresh. For a while, though, Lavinia would phone me at all times of the day or night, oblivious to things like time differences between different parts of the world.

I remember one extremely annoying one, because it woke me from a very nice sleep at around 3am in the morning. She was in Jamaica when I received a particularly garbled phone call from her. She was talking in what I suppose she thought was the local pâté, which you just can't do with a Huntingdonshire accent – from Little Gidding, she was, Dear Hearts. Anyway, I could make neither head nor tail of it; something about some unsavoury-sounding character called Iron-Eye from Inner Babylon or somewhere, some suburb of Kingston, I suppose. I do wish she wouldn't phone me when she's been on the tango cigarettes.

I remember another occasion when she phoned me to tell me about her new posting. Geography was never really one of her strong points and she told me that she'd just been posted to, in her own words, "Somewhere behind the Urals." Well, I'd just woken up and wasn't really very with it and I told her that I hoped that she would keep herself properly clean there. It became a running joke for years.

And what was that other one that she was telling me about all those years ago? She'd tried to set up some sort of extortion racket in some place. Well, that's what the British Administration was for, Dear Hearts. Corruption is nothing new and was certainly never confined to banana republics and Communist regimes. Payment to employ, in minor positions obviously, the sons and daughters of the local worthies, or some such. Well, she wasn't really up on the technicalities of the language and tried to use certain slang words so as not to be too obvious. I mean, we were all trained to undertake our extortion duties discretely so that there would be less likelihood of any sort of publicity or any other sort of unpleasantness. Anyway, I suppose that the words she was trying to remember were 'payola' and 'mazuma' but the upshot of it all was that we couldn't for the life of us at the time understand why we started getting such large consignments of Mazola from that particular Commission instead of hard currency. Still, it all comes in useful; oil on the wheels of diplomacy and all that.

There are so many other memories that pop into my mind, Dear Hearts. We could be here all day. I mean, there was that time in the mid-1960s that she disappeared from view for a while. It turned out that she'd encountered the Krayfish Twins in some low down, Limehouse joint or other – probably lost again and convinced that she was in Belgravia – and spent a short while underground as a gangster's mole.

Then there was that time that she had her appendix taken out by that left-handed surgeon. I remember that as she came out of the anaesthetic she murmured that it was just like being operated on by someone else. Rambling again. And what was it that that dreadful Betjeman oik said about her?

"Her sulky lips were shaped for gin," or some such piffle.

Nonsense, it's always been sweet sherry or nothing with Lavinia. Well, that and the Lambeth Walk cigarettes, that is.

Another one I remember is when Lavinia was sent over to the US for a series of very high-level workshops on transcontinental mediation, set up so as to try to find ways of making the East-West divide a little less wide and frigid in those paranoid, Cold War days. Well, for some reason Lavinia wasn't expecting it to be such a strenuous assignment and, from what she said, was expecting to spend a lot of time in darkened rooms, burning incense, saying "Om!"

Of course, the silly, old fool – well, silly, young fool in those days – had got hold of the wrong end of the stick again. Or should that be the wrong end of the joss-stick, Dear Hearts? Oh, you didn't laugh. No, don't blame you.

Anyway, always one for any mystic fad, I remember her calling me one night to tell me that she'd found her chakra. Again, she'd woken me from a deep and satisfying sleep and so again I wasn't really paying attention. I suggested that she should keep quiet about it and go and see the doctor in the morning.

Funnily enough, it was I that first entered into the mysteries of meditation – I'd only intended to keep Lavinia company but, as often happened in any social dealings with Lavinia, she didn't turn up – turned out later that she had stayed at home in bed with one of her all-too-frequent post-nerve storm migraines. Anyway, as I was there I thought that I might as well go through with it, not that I was particularly bothered with that sort of guff.

And as it turned out I'm not sure whether whatever his name was – Yogi or Boo-Boo or something – actually took me particularly seriously. I began to have my doubts after he told me that I must be given a secret word, my own personal mantra, which I should say quietly to myself in my head over and over so as to induce a state of euphoric, out-of-body wellbeing. That in itself sounded quite sensible at first glance – after all, we cats all have our own very secret name that we keep to ourselves and say to ourselves when of troubled heart or mind.

What's that, Dear Hearts? What's mine? Oh, how sweet of you; I'll have a Milk Stout, thank you.

Further Adventures of Tabitha Miggins...

Well, my doubting started because the secret word he gave me was something unpronounceable – hang on; I've still got it written down somewhere for some unfathomable reason. Here it is – "Pneumonoultramicro-scopicsilicovolcanoconiosis". I spent most of the time just trying to remember what the blasted thing was, let alone how to pronounce it. Still, I discovered that being transported to a choleric plateau of ire was just as good a way of getting all the stress out of my system.

Anyway, Dear Hearts, it's all a lot of nonsense if you ask me. Funny, though, how my initials should be TM, especially since I'd always thought of them as being my trademark.

Well, that's probably enough about Lavinia for the moment – oh, hang on, before we move on, what was it she told me on the telephone last night? Oh yes, that she was going to have a bit of a makeover for the umpteenth time. Oh dear, the last time was when she had herself dyed ginger, and why a tortoiseshell should want to be ginger, I don't know.

"As an aid to the natural markings," is what Lavinia generally says. That or some other thought-free and trite rubbish.

But that's Lavinia all over, always wanting to be something she's most obviously not rather than being comfortable with her own coloration. My own coloration – classic tabby, though I say so myself – is perfectly natural and isn't there to deceive anyone, Dear Hearts, though it does on occasion deceive me into acting to type. Tabby is as tabby does as they say, and all such nonsense, as if we didn't all have free will and a brain to think with. And lucky it is too, touch wood, or we'd be a nation of uncritical morons, bound by superstition and outmoded convention. Oh dear, I'm rambling again.

Still, back to the point in paw. No sooner had she had herself dyed ginger than her fur started to fall our leaving various unsightly bald patches behind. I suggested that she go to see the quack double-quick, much as I dislike the species, to see what it was that was causing it and to find out if anything could be done. As she came out I asked her what the verdict was.

"Loose fur," she replied.

"Sounds like the Devil," I said.

She didn't spot that one, so I let it go, Dear Hearts. I sometimes despair at those who don't have a little fun with our language. As you already know, I've always enjoyed cryptic crosswords, since they came in, and those rather quaint double-crostics before them. Still, that's by the by. As for Lavinia, the fur started to grow back after a while but, of course, it was tortoiseshell. Well, didn't that look odd on a ginger cat!

Oh well, only time will tell as to what she's doing this time. If we don't see her down at *The Duke* for a month, then we'll all know that whatever it is has all gone wrong, as usual, and that she's waiting for the colour, or the perm or whatever, to grow out. That or she's joined up and been shipped out to some war zone or other.

Oh yes, Dear Hearts, talking of war zones, there was that bad scare about Lavinia's Kevin a while back, whilst he was battling the dark forces of Islamic State by writing incomprehensible memos in his posting as a junior clerk in wherever it was – oh, I don't know, somewhere even more unpronounceable than my secret mantra. I remember reading about that poor operative that was kidnapped over there, not realising that it was the same place to which Kevin had just been posted. Indeed, that Kevin was the replacement.

Well, as to the unlucky operative, shortly after he'd gone missing, a letter had arrived back at the Consulate, containing his left ear tip – they'd used pinking shears by the look of it – along with the message that more parts would arrive by each post unless the terrorists' demands were met and that it was our fault, not theirs, because we'd completely ignored their first missive in which they'd laid out their grievances and listed their demands in *very neat* handwriting. Well, what with such an efficient local postal service as they enjoyed, the parts continued to arrive twice a day – a set of whiskers here, a tail there. Quite soon bits arrived that the poor thing couldn't so easily do without. At least, Dear Hearts, they ended up with a complete set for burial.

A couple of weeks after the last part arrived the Consulate received a quite apologetic letter from the terrorists. Basically, they'd just found the letter in which they'd stipulated their demands hidden behind the clock on the mantle-piece. The cleaner must have put it there, the letter explained, and they'd all just assumed that someone else must have posted it. The letter also mentioned, almost in passing, that they'd kidnapped another of our chaps and were going to give it another go, if that was alright with us. Inside was a very distinctive, furry paw.

Further Adventures of Tabitha Miggins...

Well, this was the first that anyone had realised that Kevin, the new arrival, was missing. Luckily, what the terrorists had sent was his lucky rabbit's foot – not so lucky for the rabbit, I always thought, but that's neither hare nor there. The terrorists must have cut it off thinking it was attached; which it more or less was, what with Kevin having picked up a dose of the superstitions from his mother.

Well, the biggest mistake they'd made was to send this particular letter on headed notepaper, complete with address, so our chaps went in that afternoon and rescued Kevin after a very long gun battle out of which none of the terrorists emerged alive. We never did find out what their demands were, what with the place burning down and all that.

Anyway, long before Kevin appeared on the scene, I remember that many of our contemporaries were scandalised when Lavinia started to date various non-feline fellows – for instance, our old governess, Mary Harrow, was horrified – of course, with a name like that, when she wasn't about we called her Hairy Marrow. So amusing. I remember Lavinia having a choking fit when we heard that she'd given up being a governess and had finally been and gone and married that awful Hinge chap that was always hanging about her in besotted fashion with a look on his face like a demented sheep. Can't for the life of me think what Lavinia had found so amusing about that. Pointlessly-ineffectual chap, he was to my mind. Had a squint as well.

Anyway, where was I? Oh yes, Lavinia and her non-feline beaus. Well, it didn't really make much difference because all of her relationships always seemed to end in disappointment. I remember her telling me once that she was dating a beaver to see if things would be any different. I well remember her on the phone a few nights later, sobbing her heart out she was, poor thing. Evidently he was just like all the otters.

Well, that's *definitely* more than enough about Lavinia for now. What else should I tell you? I mean, to be honest, everything here in Pill is very much the same as ever. Oh, I know – how about the badger cull?

Well, Clarence the Cross-Eyed Badger is still with us. We all pulled together and disguised our local badger families so that they wouldn't end up at the end of some gun-sight or other for no reason other than for a weak-in-the-head Government – a tautology, I know, Dear Hearts – to look as though it was doing something about a problem.

In fact, what we did ended up helping to save so many more badgers. Basically, we added a little rouge to strategic parts of all of our local badger friends and then told the authorities, when they came waving their guns and poking their silly noses in where they weren't welcome, that we had no badgers in Pill or the surrounding areas, thank you very much.

At which point Clarence – he uses slugs as ear plugs, by the way, Dear Hearts – wandered flatulently past with near-constant stream of verbal tics on his way to *The Duke* just before opening time. In a twinkling, eight gun barrels were raised and pointing, itchy trigger fingers well in evidence, straight at poor, old Clarence. The one with most brain, which isn't saying a lot, Dear Hearts, challenged us as to what was *that* then, if not a badger.

Well, as per my plan, we told them that he was an indigenous Somerset red panda and that they were on the protected list, and shooting even one of those would incur the wrath of the Red Panda Brigade, who had powerful lobbying rights at Westminster.

All rubbish, of course, but the wonderful thing about The Establishment is that no one really knows who or what has overt political power, or even which entities really exist. That's one of the benefits of having spent a lifetime in the inner circle, which gave me near-free access to the cat-flaps of power – in awful, modern, jargon filled business terms, you have to learn quickly, if you want to be successful in The Service, that is, how to leverage a very small amount of Zen. And I'll tell you what else, Dear Hearts, if you can get them to start up a Royal Commission on something or other, then you know you've pretty much won, because everyone will be too frightened to make anything like a decision, what with the public eye on them.

So how did this almost childish ruse save lots of other badgers, I hear you ask, Dear Hearts? Well, the local authorities got on to their gun-toting Myrmidons to warn them not to shoot if they could see any red on what otherwise looked like a badger. Well, Dear Hearts, the thing about night-sights is that anything white looks red at night. And, of course, most badgers only come out at night, Clarence being a bit different to most in aligning his innate behaviour to fit with Somerset's take on licencing hours. We just kept slapping the make-up on him, that's all.

Nutter Slater was very unkind and said that, if anything, it just made Clarence look like an elderly, gay badger with a heart condition. I won't tell you what Clarence did in Nutter's Loopy Juice by way of retaliation, whilst

Nutter was taking a 'comfort break' as I think they're called nowadays. Not that Nutter noticed anything when he returned and downed his suddenly less empty drink in one, Dear Hearts.

Anyway, to return to the point. Thanks to hardly any bullets being fired, except for the odd understandable mistake, when the occasional bored badger hunter caught site of non-black and red movement in the undergrowth and took out a fellow badger hunter – I wonder how silly one looks on arrival at the Pearly Gates when one has to admit that one was a casualty of friendly fire in a badger cull – the whole project came in well under budget in this area, so from that point of view the government must have deemed it a success, I suppose.

Afterwards, of course, there was no appreciable decease in bovine TB, as anyone could have told you. Anyway, there were a few rumours from several loose-lipped and cruel individuals that the Government was going to start culling cats next to see if that had any effect on bovine TB.

Well, I had a horrible dream that night, Dear Hearts, I can tell you – no, not the one about two pieces of coal getting married after meeting at a carbon dating agency; I really must stop eating Stinking Bishop before bed. As to the horrible dream, well we were all herded up – herding cats, I ask you; except that it was very effective – and marched into a big, windowless warehouse with pictures of happy, tumbling, laughing and wool-chasing kittens painted on the side. At which point they slammed the doors shut and turned on the gas. Thankfully, I woke up at that point and had a nip of Milk Stout to take away the awful feeling of choking that was left over from the dream.

When I settled down again, the dream continued. Even with all the cats gone there was no cessation of bovine TB and one day the government announced that experts had heard someone in the street saying that it might be *people* that passed on bovine TB. What with no other leads it had decided to go with this because it was just as likely as anything that had already been labelled as scientific fact.

Amazingly quickly, a law was passed that anyone living within a ten-mile radius of a dairy farm would be culled. Thanks to some oversight at the bill reading stage this ended up including all the farmers and their families. And then, of course, they discovered how many dairy farms there were within a ten-mile radius of most city centres and so the culling of people carried on.

Isn't it funny that in every country there are always plenty of people who are willing – indeed, keen – to slaughter others at the Government's behest. Of course, what with the Armed Forces having been recently decimated by cutbacks, much of the work was outsourced to Al-Qaeda, IS and the CIA – and jolly hard it was, Dear Hearts, to tell one of these groups from the other on casual inspection. And still, of course, there was no appreciable decline in bovine TB.

My dream came to an end just at the point that a surviving expert had announced a breakthrough and that they'd discovered, once and for all, that bovine TB was contracted from other cattle. I suppose that the clue might have been in the name. So, as I woke up in good time for my shift, they'd started culling the cattle, what with there being little need for them now that there weren't many people left in the UK, other than the Royal Family, the government and its advisors, the Army, Al-Qaeda, IS and the CIA.

Anyway, my dream aside, the only real problem was that the national press publicised our little red panda fantasy along with our assertion that there were no badgers in or around Pill, at which point we had a very unwelcome influx of Wombles, coming from all directions to take over any old badger setts that they could find.

What's that, Dear Hearts, don't the Wombles live on Wimbledon Common? Well, I only wish that they did. They were eventually evicted from their traditional home there. A regular crime spree, that's what they were. Pretended that they only took things of no value; and perhaps they did to start with, but they soon revised their definition of rubbish to include only things that could be fenced lucratively so, effectively, that was newspapers out and Rolex watches in. Indeed, anything of value that wasn't firmly enough nailed down. Turn away for a second and it would be gone. They say that the Invisible Womble was quite useful there. Talking of which, what was that rubbish I read on the Interweb thingy the other day about the Invisible Womble only ever appearing in one episode? I mean, how on earth could anyone tell? Anyway, that aside, it was always said that if you shook hands with a Womble – not that they ever did anything to warrant such a thing happening – then you had to count not just your rings afterwards but also your fingers.

They were all smiles in front of the cameras, but a very different kettle of fish off air. A nasty lot, especially that Tomsk – he played dumb but it was all crafty-dafting. Then, of course, some of the younger ones started to dabble in foxtrot cigarettes and worse during their pop star phase, repapering hotel rooms with old copies of *The Times*, throwing rocking chairs into swimming pools and so on. I mean, everyone of a certain age remembers Orinoco and Keith Moon getting dressed up as Mussolini and Clara Petacci and going on a drunken ramble in the West End. Of course, their agent spun it as a harmless publicity stunt. And, whilst I'm at it, Dear Hearts, from what I hear, that Madam Cholet is no better than she should be, if you get my drift, and is about as French as I am.

Anyway, they took to the travelling life because nowhere would have them – when they turned up here, they were rather surprised to find that all of the local badger setts were full of extremely annoyed and well-armed Somerset red pandas. There was a pitched battle and the Wombles, a cowardly lot when it comes down to it, decided to move on to somewhere more docile. Besides, there was very little left for them to steal after they'd been in the area for a day or so.

It's funny that their motto should have been 'Make Good Use of Bad Rubbish' because our take on their moving on included a couple of the same words with "Good Riddance to" added in there somewhere. I'll leave it to you to work that one out for yourselves, Dear Hearts.

I recently heard that they've started to play at folk festivals around the country, riding on the nostalgia ticket – and if you think that I'm going to stoop to doing the obvious nostalgia joke, then I'm afraid you'll have to stay wanting, Dear Hearts. Anyway, that aside, I managed to catch them at Priddy this year. Their new stage act is quite fun, if you like that sort of thing – they've rewritten the words to all of their old hit songs. Risqué isn't quite the word – downright filthy is closer to the mark. But, then, that's Wombles all over for you.

Oh, hang on, Dear Hearts, perhaps all that was still part of the dream, just like the one about the Clangers' demand for gender-specific appendages in the knitting patterns and the one about Bagpuss being a funny colour because he'd eaten too many flamingos. It does get so difficult to tell sometimes, especially after one or two too many Milk Stouts, not to mention all this limburger and the like that Lavinia keeps passing on to me.

Talking of Lavinia again, there was that funny dream I had the other week about her blowing up a whole race of aliens that had come to be friends with us. Now that really was an odd one. We were all waiting outside *The Home*, on the high ground just up from the Adam and Eve water-gate, because we knew that the alien fleet would be arriving here to parley with us, though why they'd chosen Pill wasn't particularly well explained in the dream. I mean, it's mostly Yatton that the things head for. Anyway, for some reason Lavinia didn't seem to know what was going on or why we were all looking up into the sky and decided to head indoors to find something to amuse her. Well, she headed into the computer room to see if there were any games that she fancied playing and settled on a nice, retro Space Invaders one that was one of her favourites.

What no-one knew was that one of the visitor's children had been sent off earlier in the day to amuse himself whilst his parents had a pleasant chinwag with their old Colonial Companion. He'd headed down to the common room where there was one of those colourful Sunday supplements with the lead story about the Pentagon's new IT security measures. The cover was emblazoned with a header stating that the new system was "un-hackable". Well, on reading that our hero headed straight to the computer room just to see if it was true. It evidently took him about ten seconds to get into the Pentagon's military mainframe via that very same computer that Lavinia was later to choose. Then, on a whim, having given himself a nice, warm feeling by hacking into the supposedly un-hackable – the password, by the way, Dear Hearts, had been "qwerty123" – he decided to hook up the Space Invaders game with the US Central Command's Surface-to-Air Warhead Direction System, whilst he was at it. Of course, once he'd spent all of forty more seconds doing this he'd got bored and wandered off and in the space of seconds had completely forgotten about what he'd done. Children just have such short attention spans these days.

Well, Lavinia started to play the game just as the first spaceship appeared above us. As we gazed in awe, a second appeared and then a third, then a fourth, until in a few minutes, the whole sky was ablaze with light from countless ships – a whole fleet of gigantic and majestic spaceships floated high in the night sky overhead. Then, as we stood, jaws dropping at the sheer beauty of it all, one by one, the spacecraft all started to blow up. In purple.

We'd just got over the shock when Lavinia suddenly reappeared to tell us about what a wonderful time she'd just had.

Further Adventures of Tabitha Miggins…

"Guess what, everyone. I've just got my highest ever score; you'll never believe how many points I got. Go on, guess…I say, what's all this debris?"

At which point I woke up. Just in case you're interested, Dear Hearts, that one was courtesy of Jarlsberg and Blue Vinney.

Well, good heavens, I seem to have started rambling good and proper, haven't I? I'll have to tell you about a few of the other local inhabitants a little later otherwise we'll never get to the adventures, shall we, Dear Hearts?

Anyway, I've got to stop here because it's time to warm my milk ready for an early night so that I can be up bright and early to bake my daily loaf and start my shift on the Pill Ferry. I wonder if I'll have an adventure tomorrow.

2. From home to home

Do you know, Dear Hearts, that there's nothing nicer than spending the long, dark, winter nights in the snug at *The Duke*? It's like a home from home as I sit and knit, warming myself next to the fire. On those long, dark, winter nights – you know, those ones that I've just alluded to – the curtains are drawn. But everything else is real.

Oh, you didn't laugh, Dear Hearts. On reflection, I don't think that I blame you, though it seemed very funny when old Buster Bailey came out with it in the snug, last night. Still, that's enough of levity. Adventures are on the way, but I thought that first I'd do just a very short chapter – think of it as the merest aperitif before the main course – to let you know what's been happening on the home front.

Well, I've bought my cottage again. Twice, in fact. Once when it was first built back in the mid-eighteenth century – number 1, Peggle Cottages, it was called then long before the coming of the railway – and again in the 1900s. Such a shame that I'll have to sell up again in 1847 and 1962, but there's documentary evidence of others living there and there are only so many liberties that you can take with reality. Talking of the railway, the fact that it was built in the first place was mainly because of me, but that's another story and one that I'll leave until another time.

What's that, Dear Hearts? Why have I bought the cottage again? And again? Well, there's so much money coming in from my Pill Brewery shares and my commissions for various articles of clothing from most of the world's pirates from the late eighteenth century, not to mention winning some money on the gee-gees last week when Alfresco came in first at 200-1 – it always does to back outsiders, Dear Hearts – that I thought that I ought to actually do something with it other than just move it from account to account so as to get the best interest rates possible. Indeed, I can't even spend the interest without some slight extravagance.

I have to admit that it can be quite fun living back in the 18th century, though I generally hop back to modern times when I need to use the smallest room. I was there in 1755 when an awful prig called John Wesley came lording it here on his horse – no, I mean that I was in the 18th century, not the smallest room, Dear Hearts. Do keep up!

Further Adventures of Tabitha Miggins...

Now, I've got nothing against the horse, very tidily done up with neatly-groomed fetlocks and all, but the rider seemed to think that we were all here to be preached at. Lots of silly ideas about temperance and the like. And what a place to choose, a village with, at that point, twenty-seven public houses, and a sea-hardened set of hard-drinking inhabitants. Well, he didn't stay long, especially after a badly-aimed shot from one of the apprentice hobblers took his hat off.

What's that, Dear Hearts? That doesn't sound badly-aimed? Well, he was aiming for the chap's nose.

As for the Wesley oik, I'm surprised he didn't get lynched. Anyway, he scarpered somewhat sharpish and shouted over his shoulder that he was jolly well going to tell everyone what he thought of us and that he was going to put it in his journal for posterity as well. Silly sod.

What's that, Dear Hearts? What did he write in his journal? Well, I was just about to tell you. I'll just get the volume down from the shelf. Ah, here it is:

"I rode over to Pill, a place famous from generation to generation, even as Kingswood itself, for stupid, brutal, abandoned wickedness."

Well, Dear Hearts, I know what you're thinking. Who'd have thought that he would write such nice things about us? Zebadiah Cox, the Landlord of *The Red Lion*, edited out the bit about Kingswood and had it carved on a nice piece of sea-smoothed driftwood that had conveniently meandered in on the morning's tide. It hung proudly over the big mirror behind the bar for well over a century.

Anyway, talking of *The Red Lion*, I was having a bit of a natter with my old neighbours in the snug there last night back in 1787 when there was quite a kerfuffle outside on the creek. It turns out that the Revenue had come down quietly and in force from Bristol to have a quick look over one of our regular visitors, the *Young Fanny*, a Dutch galliott that had just that second pulled in on the late tide.

Well, someone somewhere must have blabbed is all that I can think. It didn't take the Revenue long to find the six ankers of brandy and the couple of bales of tobacco hidden under the catch of fish that the boat was officially bringing in. Well, smuggling is all very well – it's pretty much what makes the world go around here in Pill – but I for one couldn't stand buying any contraband that filled the whole house with the smell of fish for weeks on end. Of course, if you like smoking a pipe-full of mackerel-flavoured tobacco, then be my guest.

Things are normally a bit quieter on the smuggling front and the local Revenue man tends to turn a blind eye to most of it. In fact, there's a bit of a macrobiotic relationship going on between the Revenue chap and our smugglers. For instance, when he's short of money, which is quite often, what with pay being performance-based for those in the Revenue Service, the locals lead him to various stashes of 'smuggled' goods – always so badly hidden and always on common land – so that he can claim the reward based on the value of the goods, as is usual practice at this point in time. The first thing he always does when he's been paid his Revenue fee is to buy everyone involved a very large drink. It all seems to work very well. And it's funny how the goods that he 'finds' always seem to be just the ones that the local smugglers have had a bit of trouble selling.

What's that, Dear Hearts? Why do I use *The Red Lion* instead of *The Duke*? Well, *The Red Lion* is so much closer to the Ferry slipway, though I might just as easily have been at *The Waterloo Inn* or the dear, old *Seven Stars*, to be honest. Or *The Duke*, of course.

Anyway, as to owning the cottage again up until 1962, well it's so convenient for the amateur dramatic society that I've recently joined. I'd always wanted to tread the boards again after getting a small taste at 'varsity in *The Importance of Being Earnest*; I played Lady Bracknall, of course, though I kept getting the lines wrong and heaven knows the ad-libbing that the rest of the cast had to do to get past my constant declamations of "A Knitting Bag!" Great fun watching other actors panicking in front of a paying audience, I'll have you know, Dear Hearts, taking light comedy so seriously. Silly sods.

Well, I didn't want to join any of the contemporary societies that constantly seem to be obsessed with modern rubbish written by people with no talent. Either that or they insist on putting their minimal acting skills into staging the worst sort of unfunny musical comedy. Well, eventually I found what I was looking for but it does mean that I have to go back to 1956 every Thursday evening to rehearse *Murder in the Cathedral* with the Tickenham Players. Hence it's nice to have a home to go to if I'm feeling a little too washed out after immersing myself in character to think myself back to my proper time for a bit.

Further Adventures of Tabitha Miggins...

Do you know, Dear Hearts, that it's funny that I should have brought up *Murder in the Cathedral* because it's reminded me of a whole stack of correspondence that I had with the chap that wrote it. In fact, I was responsible for a great deal of his work being as accessible as it is. When I first met him on one of my jaunts back in time – I forget which – he was wasting far too much time in asking advice from that awful Pound chap, despite the fact that old Ezra had clearly gone off the boil good and proper, if not off his rocker. I mean, suggesting all those bits in foreign languages that no-one in their right mind understands. Of course, some of it remained, but I managed to persuade dear, old Tommy to cut reams of the stuff out.

How nice of the dear chap to leave all his effects to me when he popped off. There's a suitcase full of mostly unpublished stuff under the bed. Most of it nonsense, of course. Lucky no-one else has ever read it. He'd probably have been locked up. But it means I got my old letters back. All five hundred or so of them.

Ah, here's the suitcase. Now let's just put in my paw and pull one out at random. Right, let's see what I've got. Oh yes, Dear Hearts, I remember nipping back to my cottage in early 1917 to post this one.

T.S. Eliot Esq.,
C/o The Oxford and Cambridge Club,
71-77 Pall Mall,
London.

1, Railway Cottages,
Sunnyside Mews,
Pill,
Somerset.

26 February, 1917.

What ho! Tommy, old chap,
I hope things are well with you. At least, as well as they can be - I told you that you'd regret marrying her. And I'd get her to give that so-called philosopher chap's society a bit of a miss if I were you.

Anyway, as to the other matter, you'll find that things will start to calm down in a day or so if you get that recipe I cabled you yesterday mixed up at the local chemist's. Nothing can be done about the hobnailed lung, I'm afraid, other than giving up the gaspers, not that you will, but my little remedy should sort out the hobnailed liver. And lay off the gin for a bit is my advice, again, not that you'll take it.

And don't think to yourself that I've ever needed such a drastic potion! Good Heavens, the very thought; I got that one from my friend, Lavinia; you know, the one I've told you about - that's right, the one that came up with "Codpiece filled with straw, alas" for that very odd poem that you've thankfully put on a back burner. I'd put it on a Bunsen burner myself. Not the remedy, I don't mean - that'd probably take the entire block out - but the poem.

Anyway, those lines you're struggling with for that 'J Arthur Rank' poem, or whatever it's called; here are my suggestions:

"In the room the new men come and go, Tolkien, Orff, Michelangelo"

That'll do nicely - even though you've probably never heard of the first two quite yet. Don't worry, it will be something for literary critics to worry over in twenty or so years. You know, a how-did-you-know-that-they'd-be-so-important-later sort of thing? And just you keep that idiot, Pound's nose out of it. Haven't got a clue what he's going on about half the time. Just keep it simple and in English for goodness sake. I mean, what's with all this highbrow stuff anyway? Why don't you team up with the Crazy Gang - not that they exist yet - or knock out a few limericks for once? You know the sort of thing? How about:

There was a young man from St Louis,
Who poems were pretty much useless,
He lived on his wits,
But fell on his...

...oh, no, perhaps not a good idea after all, Dear Heart, thinking about it. Anyway, I'm having a bit more trouble with the other bit. Best attempt so far is:

"I grow old... I grow old... I shall wear the bottoms of my trousers an inch above my sensible, Oxford brogues"

It still needs a bit of working on...oh, I know, how about:

"I grow thin... I grow thin... I shall wear the bottoms of my trousers tucked in"?

And I don't get that sudden reference to fruit at all. I think you should change that bit to:

Further Adventures of Tabitha Miggins...

"Do I care to make a speech?"

That's it for now. Be good, Dear Heart. Oh, and probably best not to sit too near any naked flames for ten or so minutes after you've had Lavinia's cure. Don't cough, either. And don't light a gasper, for Goodness' sake.

Yours sincerely,
Tabitha.
(Pawprint under name)

Well, we kept in touch right up until the end even though in the last few years there was a certain amount of cooling in our friendship, perhaps because I didn't finally appear in *Old Possum*. I can't think how the omission came about, because I distinctly remember sending the chap something that Lavinia had penned in an idle moment, suggesting that it might give him some ideas, and he'd seemed quite pleased with it at the time. How did it go again? Ah, here it is:

The wonderful thing about Miggins,
Is Miggins is no fool,
Her head's a-whirl of ideas,
Her paws a frenzy of wool.
Duty, duty, duty first,
Before she would think of fun,
And the wonderful thing about Miggins is,
There couldn't be more than one.

Reminds me of something or other, though I can't think what offhand. Oh yes, and there was that one that I felt the urge to write after I'd caught the wrong train at Temple Meads and headed down the branch on the other side of the river. It was all so run down and depressing that I just had to go back in time and spend a day going up and down the line in 1956. Well, what a difference – the hustle and bustle of it all in those days. The highlights were a proper cup of tea – one that you could stand the spoon up in – in a proper buffet at Stapleton Road, listening indolently to all the tannoy announcements, and a nice sit down in front of a blazing fire in the booking office at Shirehampton before I headed down to catch the Ferry back across the river. Long before I or the Captain were around, of course. It was funny running across with no Ship's Cat in evidence.

What's that, Dear Hearts? How does the poem go? Oh, good heavens, I'd forgotten the whole point of this, hadn't I? Well, I'm not really much good at this sort of thing, but here it is for what it's worth. Lavinia suggested on first hearing that it was a fairly harmless piece of doggerel, which I didn't necessarily agree with. Harmless catterel, more like. Anyway, here goes:

The Severn Beach branch in happier times,
By Tabitha Miggins (aged 96 and a third without taking into account various excursions, by train and otherwise)

> *From Temple Meads we steam gently out,*
> *Then on with further compunction,*
> *Nearing the first suburban station,*
> *Past Dr. Day's Bridge Junction.*
>
> *First Lawrence Hill, then Stapleton Road,*
> *Alight here to change for South Wales.*
> *Montpelier, Redland, Clifton Down,*
> *Alight here to shop in the sales.*
> *Sea Mills, Shirehampton, Avonmouth,*
> *Alight if your pleasure be ships.*
> *Then up the Severn estuary,*
> *For Severn Beach and fish and chips.*

All jolly good fun and it goes tumpty-tumpty-tumpty-tum as near as makes any difference. Well, that's about it for now, Dear Hearts. After all, I haven't been living back in either of my new purchases for long, so there's not really that much to tell you about yet. I'm sure there will be more once I've spent rather more time there. So, on to the adventures we go, Dear Hearts.

3. Up the creek without a waddle

Life is full of sadness, Dear Hearts, and I think that it must be time to give you some bad news. It's all part of growing up and being British and I don't mind telling you that, when it happened, we all shed some not-so-quiet tears. So what is this bad news? Well, I suppose I'd better just let you have it like it is, though you might need a bit of a stiffener first.

What's that? Hadn't I promised to tell you about some of my recent adventures? Well, yes, but it won't hurt to wait until the next chapter, will it? I'll tell you what, Dear Hearts, if you'll indulge me for this chapter, then I'll spend the rest of the book having adventures. How does that sound?

What's that Dear Hearts? Do I promise? Well, to be honest, it's my book and I'll do what I like, but...oh, all right, I promise.

What's that, Dear Hearts? Why have I got my paw behind my back? Have I got my fingers crossed? Don't be silly, Dear Hearts, cats don't have fingers.

Anyway, back to the bad news. Have you had that stiffener? Well, here we go. Willard, I'm sorry to say, Dear Hearts, has been taken from us since my last literary outing. It was a sad blow for the whole community and, of course, absolutely devastating for his intended – I mean, she was there when it happened and can still barely bring herself to talk about it.

Such a void he's left behind him. Percival tried to take over the protection racket – after all, someone had to run it. He did his best but he just doesn't seem to have a confrontational bone in his body. Besides, Willard was a particularly hard act to follow. Percival's off sick at the moment – in fact he's gone back to the Bahamas for a spot of warmth along with his recuperation. I don't think he'll ever get over having to say, "Terribly sorry about this, old chap, but you've missed a payment, so that'll be £12.50 or I'll have to slit you up a treat," to many of his avian friends. Not that they minded, of course. They all know that it's just a job.

And whilst I think about some of our new friends from the last book, Belinda and Fernando aren't out and about much thanks to helping out the Tickenham Ladies Knitting Circle, which has taken on yet another completely mad commission. They're all knitting a life-sized depiction of the Charge of the Light Brigade for the Failand Carnival, complete with exploding hussars and horses. Sticky Paws is helping with the explosive charges, evidently, which means that fertiliser sales must be up again in the district. I do hope that they've booked extra St John's Ambulance reserves just in case.

Anyway, back to the protection racket, what we've done is to open a building society account and everyone is voluntarily paying in their protection money each week; and when we've got enough we're going to book the Somerset Paddies and have a jolly good knees-up. Well, we'll call it a May Fair, or some such, to legitimise it. We'll all raise a glass to Willard and drink to his now sadly curtailed though previously protracted perseverance in pursuance of protection of Pill's plumed populace.

Still, alliteration aside, I'm rather shying from the point at hand, Dear Hearts, which is how Willard, hale and hearty as he was, was taken from us so suddenly. Well, it happened in his sleep, otherwise I suppose it might have been a lot more unpleasant.

The door was kicked down and before he knew it, the rozzers had pulled him out of bed, warned him of his rights and bunged him, wing-cuffed, into the back of the Black Maria. They knew their stuff, I must say, and didn't give him a chance to get hold of his trusty flicknife. Nor the other one. Nor the other one.

It was all down to that incident at the Women's institute the previous weekend. How was Willard to know that the person giving the prizes for the best Jitterbug-a-go-go-goch was the Chief Constable of the area? I mean, he didn't have his uniform on, nor even his hat, though, as dear Vivian was wont to say, that just makes them look like postmen. Well, when postmen were properly dressed, that is. I don't know what the world's coming to, allowing posties to wander around half-naked. Wearing shorts. I ask you, is that professional behaviour? I think not. Bring back some discipline, that's what I say.

Where was I? Oh yes, well, I think that someone really should have tipped off the Chief Constable to give the first prize to Willard based on the premise that he'd just take it otherwise. Which is indeed what he did. The Chief Constable showed all the wrong traits in my mind in trying to grab the prize back so as to give it to the original recipient; at which point Willard got busy with the old flicknife.

I know what you're thinking, Dear Hearts. You thought that Willard wasn't allowed in unless he'd 'detooled' with the hatcheck girl first. Well, he did for a while, but the silly baggage used Willard's finest blade to do those awful marquetry pictures of hers so as to keep her occupied whilst the dance was going on.

Of course, the next time Willard tried to use it on some specimen or other that was a bit slow in coughing up the old dinero it was all blunted and hardly any use at all. And I will say this for Willard, he is an artist with that knife. Never a frayed edge. Well, on this occasion the gash was all ragged. He had to apologise and even let them off payment for a fortnight, and that will never do. No, Willard soon started taking two knives with him; one rusty, old one to leave with the hatcheck girl and a good one, well-hidden, just in case.

Well, when it came to the court proceedings it was all a put up job, I'd say. I thought it almost ironic that such an ardent fan of rock 'n' roll, and a duck to boot, should be up in front of the DA. Oh, you didn't laugh, Dear Hearts. How about if I change that to up in front of the beak? Oh well, never mind. Gentle humour has obviously become a victim of all this brash, long-haired, alternative comedy. Give me Joyce Grenfall and Stanley Holloway any day of the week – or dear, old Freddie Grisewood, though I don't suppose that anyone remembers *Spelling Bee* now. How I used to look forward to that, back in the days when television meant only one channel and not much more in the way of programmes. More gentle times, don't you know? Sorry, Dear Hearts, where was I?

Oh yes, in court. Well, as things turned out, the defence didn't have a leg to stand on. We all did our best on the perjury front, but we didn't know about the recent installation of CCTV at the WI and our loquacious pleas fell on unsympathetic, official ears. We all enjoyed the CCTV footage, though. Such a treat to see a senior policeman with his tie in tatters and his trousers around his ankles after Willard had cut his belt off.

Now, don't get me wrong, I have nothing but respect for our glorious boys in blue. Indeed, I'm all for law and order and I think that our local bobby is an absolute pillar of the community. It's pomposity that I detest, and the chief inspector is a prize specimen in this regard. And fat too. Stick him back on the beat so that he can burn off some of that lard and reconnect with real people is what I say.

Well, there I go again, Dear Hearts, and don't even think about getting me going about children in public houses or we'll be here all night.

Anyway, now we come to it. Back in court, the judge said, in the summing up, that Willard was mallardjusted and needed a short, sharp shock. Six months he got. Still, I visit every week and bribe the guard to let me pass over a four-pack of Babycham and giant hipflask of brandy.

He's doing quite well inside, to be honest. It didn't take him long to get another protection racket going, and even the warders pay into it. Sensible people. Well, I just wouldn't want to be the Chief Constable when Willard comes back into circulation, that's all. Oh yes, whilst I think of it, the WI has organised the Dalai Lama for next year's prize giving. I think I'll just have a word with him in advance. Besides it will be about time by then that Willard got first prize again.

When we arrived back from court there was a very conspicuous empty seat in the snug and I was touched that no-one attempted to sit in it in Willard's absence. The Captain and I had had to do a bit of nautical piggery jokery so as to run the Ferry all day even though we'd been in court throughout – can't let down our customers, you know – and we both had a bit of a thirst on when we appeared at opening time.

Now that's a curious phrase, 'opening time'. Just like lunch time for lorry drivers, it's a bit of a moveable feast here in north Somerset. Opening time generally tends to coincide with the appearance of the first customer.

Well, Nutter Slater was in good form that evening, and quite lucid for a while. At one point he insisted that he'd once been bitten by an allegory on the banks of the River Avon. He even went so far as to show a distinctly disinterested snug the supposed marks. He followed that up by claiming to have once accidentally stood on the Bristol Mermaid's tail and to have got away with it, which certainly isn't likely. Many's the time we hear a shout from the four ale bar along the lines of, "Yer, watch me tail, mind!" often followed-up by a thwacking sound as the perpetrator gets to learn a short, sharp lesson and one often notable for a certain brief hiatus in consciousness. Nice gel, apart from the tattoos and the shaven head, that is, but definitely a bit quick with the old left hook.

Anyway, fishy stories aside, Clarence, in-between numerous 'bog offs' and 'up the clumps', had once asked Nutter what he'd done before he retired. I was curious to hear this as well. I mean, we all know that he spent his disreputable youth in the Merchant Navy, terrorising seaports around the world, but we don't know anything about what he did when he got too old to cut it on the high seas.

Well, it seems that it was the same, old story. Once on dry land he never could fit in and just had a succession of menial jobs. He said that it didn't matter how hard he worked, he was always sacked for some reason or other. In fact he mentioned one particular instance, where he was sacked despite, as he said, "Working flat out." On closer examination it seems that he'd been found asleep under the counter, whilst on duty. As with all of Nutter's assertions, there is generally a grain of truth amongst what can best be called the perceptual flotsam and jetsam. What nice names those would be for sibling kittens, don't you think, Dear Hearts? I'm so sorry, there I go again.

Anyway, back to today, old Nutter had been in obvious pain all day in court and even the Gordano Valley Loopy Juice didn't seem to be touching it. It was evidently the 'old trouble' flaring up again and sitting down seemed to be causing severe problems.

I remember the last time that it all flared up and all the kerfuffle surrounding those suppositories that our idiot GP prescribed him. He'd complained at the size of the capsules and asked us how he was supposed to swallow anything that large. Well, Dear Hearts, the look on his face was priceless when we told him that he wasn't supposed to swallow them. It took a good few seconds for the enormity of that to filter through said perceptual flotsam and jetsam; you know, Dear Hearts, the one to which I've just alluded. Well, off to the WC he'd gone to take his first dose and none of us knew quite where to look when he came back with a startled look on his face. Well, we all knew what he had just had to do and we were all trying very hard not to giggle at the thought of whatever manoeuvres he'd had to do to get the job done in the tiny cubicle. Just the bruised forehead told a multitude of stories.

Anyway, he stood there with a sort of dishevelled dignity, taking in everyone in the snug, before declaiming loudly:

The deeply-dreaded deed be dun,
I've shoved the sodding thing up me bum.

Still, back to this particular evening. Wincing somewhat as he went on, Nutter told us his theory about old Marzo Tyning, who was nodding into his Loopy Juice at his seat at the bar and didn't look as though he would last much longer this evening. Nutter was of the opinion that when he was young – Marzo, that is, Dear Hearts; you've got keep up, you know – he'd gone to sleep with his head under the pillow, hiding from Big Eric or some other imagined monster that his parents had threatened him with if he wasn't a good boy, which, of course, he hadn't been. At which point the Common Sense Fairy had visited.

We watched as Marzo slid slowly to the floor burbling something incomprehensible. Not that anyone ever understood anything he said in the short periods of sobriety, to be honest. As he rambled away incoherently to no-one in particular from the floor I have to say that I couldn't see any flaw in Nutter's reasoning.

Clarence was late this evening and we were just going to go and have a look for him when we heard an unmistakable, "Bog off!" from outside the window. His arrival in the snug was heralded by the usual slight fragrance of bay rum, naphthalene and worms, along with that peculiar, almost unseizable odour of uncut silage. Good, now that Clarence was here we could all get down to some good, old-fashioned cheating at bar games.

It was after we'd packed the piglets off home after a particularly energetic game of backgammon that I returned to my seat next to Clarence and heard Nutter complaining to Ralph, the landlord, that his new toothpaste tasted awful. There was a pause, before he added that, to be fair to the toothpaste, at least his gums had stopped bleeding.

He had got to that stage known as 'racing against closing time' and was knocking back the Loopy Juice at a rate of knots. It has always pained me that Nutter, although he drinks to abandon – well, somewhat beyond abandon, thinking about it – doesn't really seem to enjoy his drink. Well, I'm sure you can't enjoy something at that speed. I would imagine that just keeping it down was quite a feat. The best that could be said was that at least it must have helped to keep his ears free of germs, if rendering them somewhat sticky. Anyway, I thought that the time had come to talk to him about his uncouth and unfeasibly-fast drinking habits.

"Dearest Nutter," I began, "One must savour the rare vintage, not down it drunkenly with the rim of the mug above the eyes, obscuring, as it does, the muddy prospect of the Avon beyond, and the Dalek, let's not forget – well, if it wasn't dark, that is. Not to mention getting your Urals all wet." But by the time I'd finished saying this, he'd already bought and half-drained another quart.

And then he started singing. Oh dear, it was the one about Demolition Dinah, the Picton Street Punk. Well, based on the lyrics she must have been quite an interesting girl, is all I can say. I must ask Lavinia what half of it means one of these days.

I walked him home that evening – he only lives four doors away, but it took the best part of twenty minutes to get there. No wonder cider drinkers always seem to be so thin; we must have done well over a mile in that time. I suggested, once we had definitely got to the door for good and all this time, whether he wouldn't prefer drinking something rather less toxic than Loopy Juice, such as a nice glass of Milk Stout. As to that suggestion, he surprised me with quite a lucid piece:

"Don't tell *I* that ale's superior,
I won't swallow the hop-filled bait.
Drink up thy cider, good or inferior,
And never, ever bother to discriminate."

The unexpected clarity of diction was rather spoiled by the curious sight of Nutter trying to get his front door key and the lock to coincide. Well, trying to get his front door key and his front door to coincide, to be honest. Eventually, I felt that I had to point out that his door hadn't been locked and was already wide open with his long-suffering wife watching the entire spectacle from within.

Meanwhile, what with standing idly by as he tried to miss both door jambs a few times, a couple of things I'd heard earlier in the evening managed to join themselves up in my mind in good, old Koestlerian fashion so, whilst saying goodnight, I asked if I could use the smallest room. I didn't really need it, of course, I always take advantage of the WC at *The Duke* – after all, you never know whether or not there might be a time-consuming adventure or two before you arrive home – but I digress.

Well at first, there was a certain amount of confusion as Nutter showed me the cupboard below the stairs. Not one for euphemisms, is old Nutter, especially not in the current state. Still, once his wife had shown me to the right room, I quickly found and switched around the tubes of toothpaste and pile ointment.

He seemed to be in much less discomfort the following evening, though he averred that his gums were bleeding again. A short while later a terrible air pervaded the snug and I glanced sideways at the other inhabitants. I mean, Clarence was outside with his pipe at this precise moment, so it couldn't be him.

I suddenly realised that they were all looking sideways at me. Good Heavens, how could they think such a thing?

At that moment, the culprit burst out laughing. Just like at school, the naughty ones always give themselves away if the silence goes on for too long. It was Nutter, of course.

"I dun that gert, big, smelly guff," he sniggered, looking well pleased with himself.

The atrocious odour aside, for the moment, I felt that I couldn't let him get away with this mutilation of the English language.

"No," I replied, correcting his grammar, "It is '*I did* that *great*, big, smelly guff,'"

He looked at me for a moment and said, "Oh no you don't, Miss Tabitha, you in't takin' the credit fur 'ee. It wur I dun 'ee!"

And to prove it he did another.

Three seconds later he was the only one left inside and even he was out in ten. We had to send in Clarence, whose olfactory senses have long since gone, to open the windows. I do wish that the cider drinker's farewell to his guts, if you'll pardon my mentioning such a crude and unregulated part of the body, wasn't quite so prolonged, Dear Hearts.

Talking of a cider drinker's farewell to his guts, if you'll pardon me again, Dear Hearts, we're running out of Adge Cutler gigs to go and see. He only did a finite number, of course. Well, we have to stand at the back now because we're already standing at the front. All except Nutter, of course, who goes and plays simple-to-pick-up drinking games with himself. We once brought the wrong one home for a week or so, not that anyone, Nutter included, noticed.

Whilst I think of it, what was it that dear, old Nutter came out with last week? Oh yes, I remember. He said that he wanted to see Imperial measurements pegged to Stirling and metric ones pegged to the Euro so that if the Pound was strong you would get more kilometres to the mile. Of course, he was carried off home a short while after that pronouncement.

Before I move on to some more of my friends, I must just mention one last thing about Nutter and the time that he built his own boat. I only heard this one recently, whilst sitting in the GP's waiting room with him. After his mistreatment on the NHS – no, Dear Hearts, don't get me started again – he gets nervous about his visits so one or other of us goes and keeps him company whilst he waits.

On this occasion, whilst we noted impatiently that although already well passed the appointed time, there were at least six people still in front of us, Nutter got out his lunch from one of the numerous carrier bags that he always seems to have stuffed in every pocket. A creature of habit is Nutter and his lunch always consists of a banana and a single Satsuma – not enough to keep a mouse alive, I'd say, but I suppose that there must be at least some extra nutrition in his fifteen or so daily pints of Loopy Juice. Anyway, and rather curiously to my mind, Nutter always refers to his midday meal as 'Der Führer's lunchbox' – I haven't got a clue why, Dear Hearts, have you?

Anyway, what was it that Nutter told me in the waiting room, I hear you ask? Well, I'm coming to it by degrees, Dear Hearts. It's one of those narrative tricks us writers use to heighten anticipation. Or had you forgotten all about there being any story at the end of this? Oh, you had forgotten. Well pay more attention!

Well, here's the story he told me. It says quite a lot about Nutter and his family to my mind. Evidently, shortly before I arrived in Pill, Nutter told one of his sons that he was planning to build a new fishing boat in his workshop. The son – Nutter couldn't remember offhand which one it was – warned his dad that if the boat was too big, when finished, then it wouldn't get through the double doors in Nutter's workshop. Nutter thought that it would be fine but, because his son seemed so worried, gave him a copy of the plans so that said son could build a life-sized balsa wood replica so as to find out for certain. When his son had finished building the replica Nutter went around to help carry it back to test the clearance, but they couldn't get it out of the son's bedroom.

I asked him what had happened to the real boat once built, because I'd never seen him in a fishing boat – at least, not in one of his own – and he said that it was still in his own bedroom. I asked him if he hadn't learned from his son's mistake and he said that, on the contrary, he'd though that his son's idea had been sheer genius.

"How so?" I'd asked, somewhat bemused.

"Well," Nutter began, "It's so much warmer in the bedroom than that 'orrid, draughty workshop. So I built 'er thur instead."

I'm not often speechless – indeed, Dear Hearts, I'm more often drunk on words and will never be quite sober whilst I have voice – but on this occasion I really could think of nothing to say.

Eventually, just as the silence was becoming slightly oppressive, I asked him how his evening meal had been the previous day, just for something to say, really. I'd seen him haggling with the fish monger over a fairly ropey-looking piece of coley. Indeed, I mentioned that it had looked a little overripe, as it were.

Nutter's reply also says much, I think.

"Gone off? Nevur! That fish wur so fresh, you cud've eatun yur dinnur off'n et."

Luckily, he was called in at that point. The receptionist and I shared one of those looks, Dear Hearts. The fishmonger will be much worse off when dear, old Nutter pops off this mortal thingummy.

Well, that's probably enough about Nutter for a while, though I'm sure that he'll creep into the conversation again because there's always something extra to say about him. So what else is going on here in Pill? Well, there's always a lot happening on the social front. For example, I was recently somewhat amused, reading the *Failand Echo*, to find that the Failand Rambling, Orienteering and Gliding Club, or The FROG Club as they were known for short, had been forced, because of a lack of meeting space when the Church Hall was closed, to amalgamate with the Failand Table Tennis Club and the Wraxall Equine and Ruminant Spaying Enthusiasts Club.

Meanwhile, there was an argument with the gliding contingent about the tea money, so they've moved in with the Methodists, leaving the rest under the somewhat long-winded epithet, Failand Rambling, Orienteering, Table Tennis and Equine and Ruminant Spaying Club. Despite their different interests and social backgrounds, they all seem to rub along well enough together. They all learn from each other as well and it seems that you can use two table tennis bats for spaying the male of the species in many cases.

Then there was the Robin Reliant Club that used to meet at the Tickenham Women's Institute – they used to go three-wheeling all over the place. Such fun, and whilst I think of it, there are quite a few political and charitable societies dotted about as well, always on the lookout for impressionable, uncritical and tender youth to entrap. Get 'em young and you've got a tool for life. Or is that a *fool* for life?

In fact, I was unfortunate enough to answer my front door to one rather pretty, though somewhat empty-headed, young person the other morning. She knocked to ask me to sign a petition for CND or some such organisation and started off on one of those discursive talks, as these sorts of people always do, constantly coming back to the matter of "The Bomb" – yes, the sort that seems to be able to speak in capital letters when they want to get a point across but don't really have a grasp on the facts.

Well, I was in the middle of baking when the knock came and didn't really have my mind on anything more than getting back to my cakes before they burned. The young thing had just mentioned "The Bomb" for about the sixth time in less than a minute when I felt that I had to postpone the conversation to a more convenient season.

"I'm terribly sorry, Dear Heart," I said, "But I'm dreadfully busy. Can't we just drop the bomb for now?"

She crosses the street now when she sees me coming and, if she needs to use the Ferry, pretends that she can't see me. Silly, young sod!

What else is there? Well, there are always lots of short-lived hand-bell groups, singing clubs and choirs that never really seem to get off the ground, unlike the Gliding Club. And it's such a shame that the Owls of Pill only perform so infrequently, because their singing is one of the highlights of the Pill year. It's funny, though, I still can't work out which one is Carol Singers; I mean, they all look a bit butch to me.

Talking of names, there has been some oddly-inspired naming of children here in Pill recently. Why are people such sheep? I mean, last year one rather daft set of parents called their daughter Dreena. I ask you; awful name – oh, by the way, if your name is Dreena, Dear Heart, don't be upset; I mean, if you've got as far as reading age with a name like that then you obviously have something your parents didn't have and should cope well in life no matter what your name is. Anyway, the point of this is that within the year there were four more Dreenas in the area, poor mites. The reason I mention this is because the post mistress' daughter has just called her new arrival Chlamydia. So, no doubt, there will be a rash of Chlamydias before the year is out.

Talking of silly names, I finally drew up the courage to ask Nutter why number eight son was called Bugger. He said that the vicar had stubbed his toe on the font at a crucial moment during the Christening. Very accident-prone is our vicar, as some of Nutter's other children, Oh Bum, Sod It and Ow My Foot, will tell you.

Of course, not all of Nutter's children have odd names – I mean, most of them were born before the current vicar arrived. There's Enoch, for instance. In fact, talking of Enoch, I remember him going into hospital to have his tonsils out not long after I arrived in Pill. Not much could go wrong with such a common and simple operation, I hear you say, Dear Hearts, but he was put on the trolley the wrong way round by a new theatre porter and it was a short-sighted surgeon. Thinking about it, it's funny that his name should have been Enoch. That's very nearly right now.

But I digress; what else has been going on around and about? Well, there have been a few eateries and restaurants opening in the area as well, so I thought, what with my well-documented love of pizza, to go and try the Italian that had just opened in Weston in Gordano. Well, I've been there a few times already and it has to be said that the food is exemplary, but the ambiance is somewhat spoiled by them playing absolutely appalling Italian pop music.

Well, I was quite surprised on my last visit because Classic FM was in evidence rather than the usual unlistenable rubbish. Rather a nice piece as well. Definitely Vaughan Williams, but was it the revised version of the *London Symphony* or that bit of *Job* that I always get mixed up with it? I'd missed the introduction, but thought that the owner, Miguel, might have heard.

"I say, Miguel," I started, "This music is wonderful, could you tell me what it is?"

There was a pause, whilst he straightened up from putting down a plate of bruschetta on the table across the way from mine, and then he cocked his head to one side, as though listening intently to the music just to be sure of his answer before replying.

"It ees-a..." he said, puffing himself up and looking important.

"Yes?" I asked politely.
"It ees-a..." he said again, preening himself somewhat.
"Yes?" I said again.
The rest of the clientele was getting interested now.
"It ees-a..." he said yet again.
The dramatic pause was exactly the right length.
"It ees-a... the-a classical music-a. Which was-a inventeed-a een-a Eetaly-a."

Now, I could either point out the owner's rank stupidity or I could just let it ride. Well, he was a nice chap, though a musical ignoramus.

"Thank you, Miguel," I said and turned my full attention to the horse d'oevres; funny, it tasted more like donkey, though I thought that I'd better not mention this to Oatie, just in case.

What's that, Dear Hearts? Who's Oatie? Oh, of course, how silly of me; you haven't met Oatie yet, have you? And what's that? Was I really eating horse? No, not really, Dear Hearts, I was just having a bit of fun with words, don't you know. Still, people do eat horse, you know. For instance, the Belgians have been eating horse for donkey's years, or is the other way around? No, Dear Hearts, I don't mean that anyone has been eating Belgians. I think you wilfully misinterpret things on occasion, you know.

What's that, Dear Hearts? Who's Oatie? Oh, good Heavens, yes, I'd completely forgotten that you'd asked that. Well, Oatie is one of our local donkeys – so named because he likes his oats. Lovely chap, spent his entire working life on Weston beach, trotting generations of snot-begrimed children up and down the same stretch of sand. Well, it started out as sand, but there are probably rather a few more ingredients on that particular stretch nowadays.

He told me a joke about his old job once. How did it go again? Oh yes, 'What do the donkeys on Weston beach get for lunch?' Well, of course, knowing him, I said "Oats?" which rather put him off his stroke because he felt the need to explain to me in great detail that, yes, they did get a small amount of crimped oats for lunch sometimes, though it was barley straw mostly, that and hay or haylage, and that sometimes they were even given silage despite it not being suitable for donkeys because of its high moisture and protein levels along with its low pH and fibre levels. There was a lot more besides; well, I didn't realise that there was so much to feeding donkeys. Eventually, he told me that the real answer was 'half an hour.' I laughed politely because it seemed to be expected, but I still don't get that one, Dear Hearts, do you?

Anyway, I've been teaching him to read and write and he's got himself a couple of pen friends – Bruin the polar bear and Leonard the panda. I don't know much about Bruin yet, other than that his parents probably had a sense of humour and that he is, how does one say in these dreadfully PC days, equally fond of both sexes. Nutter, never one to conform to expected social standards, refers to him as Bruin the bi-polar bear. As for Leonard, we found out fairly quickly that he is mad for New Orleans-style jazz, of all things. So we've nicknamed him 'Satchmo'. New Orleans jazz is much better, to my mind, than all that later big band jazz that all just sounded the same to my ears – always the same, boring structure. It seemed to take years for someone to come along and break out of Sinatra form. I'm so sorry, Dear Hearts, I seem to be digressing again, so back to Oatie.

The curious thing is that both Oatie and Satchmo have the same rather peculiar hobby – they spend their time going around landfill sites on stilts so that they can see over the other scavengers' heads for anything worth salvaging from the tops of the piles. Every weekend, they get in touch using one of those social media thingies to see how they both got on stilting at landfills in their respective countries.

Talking of animals, I couldn't help but notice on the way over to the restaurant that there's a big sign outside Silage McSpreader's farm advertising his speciality. It shows a picture of one of his prize porkers – his best noser – and underneath is the rather amusing strapline:

If you're looking for truffle,
You've come to the right place.

I strongly suspect input from Willard on that particular front.

Oh yes, then there's that Verity Ferret, who's recently moved into the area as well. She spends a great deal of her time in several of Pill's public houses and is generally somewhat tipsy. On a tour of French vintners recently she was so unsteady on the old pins that she fell into the vat. It took quite a while for them to get her out and she kept her mouth open the whole time. She later said that, in truth, it had all been jolly, good fun. Or, as one wag on the tour with her put it, "In vino ferret arse."

Oh dear, Miguel's just put on that dreadful CD full of Italian number one hits from the early 1970s again. It makes the Bay City Rollers sound positively gifted. I do wish that he would put some imagination into the restaurant's ambience. Perhaps next time I'll try that new Cuban restaurant that's just opened in Clapton. It's called *Chef Guevara* and promises revolutionary cuisine.

Talking of music, we have a child prodigy here. Can't think of his name offhand, but what I do know, if rumour be true, is that he was still writing the last movement of his first symphony at the beginning of the premiere performance. He evidently passed the music round to the double orchestra with a couple of minutes to spare and then knocked off the encore during the standing ovation. He'd evidently got into classical music after hearing *Pavane pour une infante défunte* and had spent his summer holiday decomposing the piece to see what gave it its spark. Luckily, he realised early on that to do so would merely be to unravel it. Yes, to break something to see the constituent parts is to miss a fundamental point of the whole. The child really is a clever one, but the rule about children in pubic houses still holds true, even for gifted ones.

Whilst I think of it, he's even recently knocked out a fairly respectable blues-rock album and he's not even thirteen yet. The *Pill Mercury* – dreadful rag, can't think why I bothered reading it – referred to him as 'Pill's go-cart Mozart' and 'the pre-teen Springsteen'. Now perhaps you can tell why I don't usually bother with it.

Well, it's been a glorious day so far as I've sat writing this particular set of reminiscences next to the open window, whilst listening to *Desert Island Discs*. Just a thought, because I've always been one to challenge assumptions, but why do people always play their favourite pieces of music on *Desert Island Discs*? I mean, if I was going to be stranded on a desert island I'd much rather take a whole lot of music I didn't know. After all, why not use the experience to learn something. Perhaps even learn the Welsh nose-flute to help pass the time – a tip, Dear Hearts, don't attempt to play one if you have a cold. Anyway, back to challenging assumptions – just remember, Dear Hearts, that life begins just beyond your pink comfort blanket.

What's that, Dear Hearts? How did I know it was pink? Well, I just did, that's all.

Oh, here's some Elgar, how nice.

Talking of Elgar, a dear chap, I remember meeting him at *Kingsweston House* back in 1898 when he was in the middle of a set of variations on *Daddy Wouldn't Buy Me a Bow Wow* – always one of my favourite songs, I have to admit – and he asked my advice on some of the names that he'd chosen. Of all things he wanted to call one part *Delores O'Hara*, for reasons that remained obscure. Well, I'd just won a decent wad of dinero on a horse called *Nimrod* and just felt like commemorating the fact, so just off the top of my head I suggested that, which he seemed to like. Then there were all those other oddly-named parts – *Rabbit*, *Bognor* and *Wombat* and the like. Well, I ask you! I suggested that he make it a bit of a mystery of things and just use a few letters from the various names.

Then there was that last bit, which was a tad slow to my mind; no bite at all and not at all what you want to finish something off with. Something jolly rousing is what you need; something for people to go home whistling, so I suggested that he change the direction on the manuscript from largo to al dente.

Oh botheration, some idiot youth has just taken up position outside my window, talking incessant garbage to one of his equally idiot friends on his mobile thingummy. How vexing! Still, I'm determined that glorious music should not be submerged by the meaningless piffle of youngsters less smart than the phones into which they yammer their duck-billed platitudes. I know, I'll turn up my DAB radio using that most old-fashioned, though gratifyingly tactile of things, the knob. Pressing a button on a handset never feels to me as though I've really done something, Dear Hearts, and neither do you enjoy such fine control.

Ah, the youngster is having to speak louder so as to combat Elgar. Excellent. And what's more, I still have around 70° worth of knob turning potential left, whilst the child is already starting to sound somewhat hoarse. Let's just turn it up a bit more.

He's not going to last much longer by the look of things. I wonder when he'll have the sense to walk away rather than trying to shout louder and louder. No, he's not that gifted, I'm afraid, Dear Hearts. Let's just turn it up a bit more.

Ah, at last he's got the message – there he goes looking somewhat red in the face. Probably wandered off for a bit of a lie down I should think. And I still have 18° of knob turning potential left.

I wonder if all my ornaments ought to be oscillating in quite that way.

Anyway, before we move on, there have been a few happenings up at *The Home* to do with one of the inmates, Lilith. I knew poor Lilith well; she was a contemporary of Lavinia and myself at Kittengarten – a perfectly happy, brindled tabby, much like myself to look at. The only thing amiss with her was that she had a phobia about being picked up and petted. Well, it's such a shame that no-one told that new, ginger-haired and oddly-freckled vet about it. The last she was ever heard to say, as he picked her up as part of a routine examination, was "Please, oh please, I just can't cope – please put me down."

I couldn't help shedding some very large tears for her as we sang *Bushy Tails in the Sky* the following day. Who'd have thought that the vet would be so literal, Dear Hearts, or indeed that he should have the doings for a lethal injection ready-made and so close-handy, or that he'd be so trigger-happy?

Still, the vet didn't last too much longer himself – sat down on one of his own ready-mades a few days later, he did. Why do I always think of Marcel Duchamp at this point, Dear Hearts? Still, that's of no import, so to get back onto the point, accidental death was the verdict – though I often wonder just what it was that Sticky Paws was doing in the chap's office, fiddling with the chair as he was, just a few minutes before the accident. I just happened to be up visiting when I spotted him as I passed the door. I didn't mention the fact to anyone; poor Lilith was very popular.

The vet arrived very shortly before I moved out of *The Home* and in the short while that our paths coincided I saw enough to know that he was not a sympathetic man. I was initially quite favourably impressed when I noticed one of the titles on his book shelf, *Our Dumb Friends*. A little condescending, I thought it, but at least he was trying to understand his patients. On closer inspection, I spotted that the subtitle, in much smaller point size, was *How to Kill, Skin and Stuff Them*.

No, Dear Hearts, he got what was coming to him. We certainly didn't shed any tears and no-one sang *Bushy Tails* for him. In fact, the only two souls at his funeral, the padre excepted, were Sticky Paws and Rat-A-Tat and, although I couldn't think at the time why they had attended, I was sure that it was not for the benefit of the deceased's memory.

After the vet's accidental death, I couldn't help but notice that the book had mysteriously transferred itself to Sticky Paws' shelf. And one thing I tried very hard not to notice was that Sticky Paws' new lampshade had a pattern that looked disconcertingly like freckles. So that's what they'd been doing at the graveside; casing the joint, no doubt. I'll bet that Rat-A-Tat's spade has been very recently cleaned as well. Again, I didn't mention anything to anyone; as I said, poor Lilith was very popular.

The new vet is a very nervous, young man. He keeps checking the drug cabinet for the signs of pick locks and looks closely at his chair before he sits down. Sensible of him, I'd say. If he doesn't blot his copy book, he might be around for a while.

Further Adventures of Tabitha Miggins…

4. May Day, mayhem and Morris Men

Do you know, Dear Hearts, I think that we can wait just one, short chapter more before I start on my adventures. On the one hand it will help to keep up the anticipation, and on the other it might also give you a few nightmares along the way, no pun intended.

What's that, Dear Hearts? What pun? Oh, you don't know what the chapter is about yet, do you? Well, I thought that I'd tell you about our May Day celebrations and our illustrious Morris team – not to mention their rather sinister 'obby 'oss. Do you understand the pun now, Dear Hearts? Nightmare and 'obby 'oss? Yes, I know it wasn't a particularly good one, but you haven't met our 'obby 'oss yet, have you? Well, let's hope that you are never naughty enough that you have to.

What's that, Dear Hearts, what is our Morris team like? What's that? You've seen Morris Dancing at your local village fête and you thought that the Morris Dancers were very funny? Well, not ours. I can only describe the Pill Morris team as dastardly and motley. Oh, you still didn't laugh. No, I still can't say I blame you.

Anyway, as for describing our Morris Team, well, let's just say that those villages that book them thinking that they'll just get a spot of mildly amusing entertainment don't ever book them a second time. Indeed, they tend to discover quite quickly the meaning of a fête worse than death. I've heard of plenty where it was impossible, without close forensic analysis at least, to tell the gore apart from the WI jam from the hundreds of smashed jars left in the wake of a sea of waving sticks, jangling and the sort of unified group leg movements that cause disturbing dreams for years to come. Oh yes, and there's always the 'obby 'oss of course.

Meanwhile, and all light-heartedness aside, here in Pill we always celebrate the real May Day – by which I mean the first of the month – heralding, as it does, the end of winter and the coming of summer. Of course, we always have an extensive jollification on the May Day Bank Holiday, generally involving plenty of mostly long-forgotten traditional games and a certain amount of imbibition, if there is indeed such a word, but we have a celebratory practice run on the first of the month, no matter on which day it falls. It is one of those things that is *Important* and it explains how the May Day Bank Holiday practice run and the local school Prize Giving happened to fall on the same day.

Of course, on those few and generally far-between occasions during one's lifetime that May Day falls on the same day as the Bank Holiday – well, those really are special. I've been back to one or two just to see if all the tales I've heard in the snug had any basis in truth. What with the veracity of the stories confirmed during my first visit, I took a crash helmet the second time.

What's that? Yes, you're right, Dear Hearts, I'm wandering from the point again, so back to the story.

Anyway, Dear Hearts, it was ever so much fun when the school Prize Giving happened to be organised for the first of May. Because of the continued importance in Pill for ancient fertility rites and that sort of symbolism that manifests itself, with complete lack of subtlety, in maypoles and the like, Nutter, as leader of the Pill Morris, was invited to make a speech and give away the prizes. After the Prize Giving, he and the rest of his team had further been asked to perform for the terrified children.

Pill's school understands all about teaching children about duty and real life from an early age. Prize Giving is not supposed to be an enjoyable event and just the thought of the Pill Morris' 'obby 'oss is enough to strike terror into even the stoutest heart. The reputation of the rest of the Morris team alone probably didn't help many children to sleep in the weeks preceding the event either.

The school had also long since given up on the tradition of giving away anything as mundane as a book at Prize Giving. I mean, what was the point? They only ended up as firelighters, or worse, for those still with outside WCs and the need for paper with slightly more resilience to damp and frost than generally provided by most papièr de toilette, if you'll pardon my mentioning the product.

This year the school had bought a job lot of Sooty and Sweep glove puppets from somewhere or other, no doubt on the cheap. Nutter, meanwhile, already well-oiled enough even at this time in the morning, managed to talk for ten whole minutes without making the slightest sense and decided to dispense with the usual academic merit-based method of choosing children for prizes – indeed, it is doubtful whether he was in any fit state to read from the list of merit in any case, so it seemed sensible to deviate from tradition. I was quite surprised that he'd even managed to get up early enough this morning after what he'd blithely termed last night's "petit écroulement" – otherwise known as collapsing after twenty-three pints of Loopy Juice. Somehow, harsh reality seems so much more elegant en français, Chers Coeurs.

Anyway, when the moment arrived, Nutter shouted out so as to make the rules clear.

"If you wants a glove puppet, you gotta put yur 'and up, see?"

I have to admit to being impressed by Nutter's wit, though no-one else seemed to spot the joke. Well, up went a handful or two of hands, these representing the children that hadn't yet spotted, in the large mirror behind the Board of Governors on the stage, that the 'obby 'oss had arrived silently in the room behind them. As usual, no-one had noticed its arrival; it was suddenly just there. Well, the more observant children were too scared to move a muscle and even the Board of Governors, up on stage, behind the speaker's podium, had gone a bit quiet and one or two fiddled nervously with their ties.

Anyway, there were three more hands up than there were prizes, so Nutter ordered the children to the front and told them that he was going to let the 'obby 'oss decide which should be the lucky ones. The 'obby 'oss didn't actually do anything. It never does, and that's what is so menacing. Whilst most 'obby 'osses horse about, this one just stands still and stares at you. It seems to get right inside your head and to tell you, mercilessly, what you really think about yourself, I've been told. Also, it's almost as if it is in lots of different places at once, only no-one seems to see it move from one place to the next. It is suddenly just there, if lucky, in front of someone else.

Anyway, Nutter awarded the prizes to those that didn't widdle themselves on the spot. He said that they were either of superior moral fibre compared to their contemporaries, or so extremely stupid that they deserved the prize whatever the case. He also acknowledged that the current Morris team was made up of people with exactly those same characteristics and took the winners' names as potential future members. Note, Dear Hearts that this included girls as well as the boys – there's no gender or role prejudice in the Pill Morris team. To be honest, some of the most feared people in Morris history have been certain fondly-remembered female members of Pill's team. That's 'fondly-remembered' in Pill alone, to be strictly accurate.

Anyway, back to the story again. When it was time for the 'entertainment', I was in two minds about whether or not to stay to see the inevitable carnage as the scratch children's teams were rounded up around the Maypole. I decided, however, to make hasty tracks as soon as I heard Marzo Tyning kicking off proceedings on the accordion with the unmistakable strains of The Cornered Badger. It was obvious that the team had decided to get in some *serious* practice before the traditional May Day Bank Holiday end of dance battle. In which case, even the Board of Governors wouldn't be safe. The teachers were fair game in any case – no one likes teachers; not children, not parents, not Governors and certainly not Pill's Morris Men.

I heard later that the prize winners had been formed up into a team on their own and, even hampered as they were with the glove puppets that they'd felt compelled to put on by a silent 'obby 'oss, gave a good account of themselves. Certainly, not many other children left the field by their own effort that morning, other than those few that managed to find the 'obby 'oss staring at someone else at a crucial moment and had made a run for it. Even with those few that ran, most never made it, but instead found the 'obby 'oss silently standing sentinel-still in whatever gap in the hedge their legs had aimed them at. None of the teachers left the field under their own power.

Well, that was on the Wednesday and the May Day Bank Holiday was the following Monday. The Easton in Gordano and Failand Morris teams had been invited to perform, as was traditional, not that either ever really stood a chance. Tradition stated that each team danced over from their respective home pub, where they stable their own hobby horses, to Pill green. Note, by the way, Dear Hearts, that the other teams have to spell their hobby horses with an 'h' – well, two, to be precise; only Pill's has the right to drop its aitches and that by ancient right of conquest. And, besides, it saves on ink. I'm sorry, Dear Hearts, I nearly started to ramble off there again, didn't I? Well, back to the rival teams' public houses: *The Rudgleigh* is the home for the Easton in Gordano Morris, whilst *The Failand Inn* does for the other lot.

Now, the thing is, you see, that it is perfectly within the rules for the home team to lie in wait and set booby traps along the route. So the Pill team tends to split into two and set out early with good supply of pointed sticks and so on. The Failand team has further to dance and consequently many less than start out tend to arrive in a fit state for the contest. But even with less far to dance the Gordano team doesn't get an easy go of it because the rivalry between the Pill and Gordano teams is so much fiercer.

Well, the remains of the opposing teams, when they arrive at the green, are given two choices. One is to fight it out between themselves, and for the winner to face the reigning Pill team, or to join forces against Pill. They usually join together depending on the current status of various inter-village or family fueds but, even with two hobby horses against one 'obby 'oss, they never really last long.

There's just one thing to mention at this point, Dear Hearts, which is that there was a curious incident this year that gave me an insight into certain things that I really didn't wish to have insight into. This is how it was.

Now, the opposing teams are given a chance to freshen up before battle commences on Pill green and the chaps in the hobby horse costumes tend to use the opportunity to have a swift pint or six, so as to give them Dutch courage enough to face up to our 'oss. Well, I've never seen our own 'oss divest its costume, which is odd considering that the rest of the team is generally fairly well tanked up by this time on Battle Day and I would expect that whoever was inside the 'oss costume would also feel the need to imbibe. So I was wondering if I'd spotted that the home team was straying from the rules by having an extra person – I mean, I could see the entire team in the currently very snug snug, including the two new reserves from the prize winners, whilst at the same time our 'oss was to be seen outside staring at a terrified and crying child – one of the few, in fact, that had made it through a gap in the hedge the previous week.

Well, fair play and all that. I felt that I had to ask Nutter a question at this point.

"Dearest Nutter," I began, "I can see the whole team, so just thought that I should ask a small question about the 'obby 'oss."

Although various conversations were still going on I could somehow tell that everyone was listening. Well, it couldn't be helped – I really couldn't let the team win by cheating. Now that I'd started, I had to finish.

"The 'obby 'oss," I began again, "If you're all in here, who's out there working it?"

There was a sudden silence in the snug and Nutter trembled slightly as he struggled with how much he felt he could say. After all, when all is said and done I'm still an outsider. Eventually he spoke.

"No-one works it, Miss Tabitha," he said quietly, "It works itself."

I decided that I already knew too much at this point and forbore from asking any further questions. Still, although the gooseflesh had risen all over me, I was relieved as well. Good, so we weren't cheating – I mean, there's nothing in the rules whatsoever about aid from supernatural entities.

Still, it was worrying as well. I mean, when it comes down to it, even Willard is frightened of the 'obby 'oss, which would tend to suggest that there is something to be frightened of. Well, I always thought that it was just about frightening the children, but our 'obby 'oss frightens whole communities. As I've already mentioned, no-one ever books the Pill Morris twice. Except for Pill, of course – well, the Pill team may be the most violent Morris team in the known world and we may have the most frightening 'obby 'oss in Christendom – and elsewhere, if the origins are true – but he's *our* frightening 'obby 'oss, which makes all the difference. From a distance, at least.

And to think that, back at our very first encounter, when the thing tried to stare at me – a cat, I ask you – all I did was pat it on the nose and offer it a piece of barley sugar from my knitting bag. Well, I remember the gasp from the crowd, but I have the feeling that the 'oss was pleased. The barley sugar disappeared, at least. I for one don't have nightmares about seeing the stark silhouette of the 'obby 'oss revealed outside my window in a flash of lightning on thunder-filled nights.

Meanwhile, back to what happens when the other team has been vanquished by the Pill Morris team. The final act is that our 'oss glares at the opposing horse for a matter of seconds, at which point the opposing horse costume bursts into flames revealing the singed and quaking team member beneath. How it is done, I don't know, and I probably don't want to know.

Still, when it comes down to it I've seen some pretty inexplicable things in my travels. I always remember that chap, when I was out in India, who used to shimmy up ropes that weren't attached to anything and then disappear at the top, though he did eventually reappear in the petty assizes for breaking and entering. And then there was that chap that seemed completely comfortable lying on his bed of nails. His speciality was getting a volunteer from the audience to stand on him whilst he was lying down and then show that the needle sharp nails hadn't made even the slightest mark on his back. I was there the day he did it for the last time. He made the usual request for someone in the crowd to stand on his belly. I really do think that Ranji should have dismounted first because I don't suppose that the invitation included his elephant. Still it's a bit too late to ask now. I'm so sorry, Dear Hearts, I seem to be deviating from the point in hand again.

Back to the 'obby 'oss. It has to be said that it has been avoiding me of late. I can't think why, except that perhaps it was because of the barley wine incident. Well, the last time the Pill Morris was playing at home – just a 'friendly', rather than the May Day bash – I'd bought the 'obby 'oss a glass of the special Pill Brewery barley wine because of its liking for my barley sugar sweets. As usual with anything proffered, the liquid just seemed to disappear – I certainly have never seen it imbibe – after which the 'obby 'oss started at me glassily for a few seconds before falling sideways all of a piece off its seat and onto the floor below. It got better, of course, but by that time our team had lost for the first time ever. No hobby horse means instant disqualification. It didn't stop the team from dancing, though and it seems that Nutter's breath was enough to knock out Failand's hobby horse. The chap inside said later that he'd suddenly come over all paralytic even though he'd only had half a pint of mild.

5. Tabitha Miggins changes the course of history (by accident)

Well, Dear Hearts, here we are at last at the start of one of my more recent adventures. I've been sort of leading up slowly to this because I'm still a touch embarrassed about it all to be honest. But, well, I suppose that I'd better get it off my chest, not that I have a chest, Dear Hearts, more a sort of furry underbelly.

Well, there I go, changing the subject again. No, I have to tell you this tale. So here goes. I think I've already mentioned that I saved the entire world through changing the course of history; well, as I also mentioned, it was all my fault that the world needed saving in the first place because I'd already changed the course of history once through a slight misadventure.

I think I mentioned in my first book, how worried I was about the impulsive way in which Pill's inhabitants casually played around with the fabric of space and time, gallivanting off all over the place and doing pretty much what they wanted without much caring about history and all that malarkey. Well, nothing much ever seemed to come of it and time always seemed to heal itself and pop you back where you should be, so I started using the local amenities in time and space to my own advantage as well.

And, of course, since I learned how to move myself around without even having to resort to the time gates – I'll tell you about that in a little while, Dear Hearts – I suppose that I've been gallivanting off all over the place on a daily basis. I mean, whelks from Bideford Bay during 1734 are the best I've ever tasted. I've been there over a thousand times between the end of May and the middle of September of that year. The locals haven't had a look in. I wonder what the Whelk Man thinks of me. From his point of view, I turn up for more every five minutes. It's getting quite hard to schedule visits without bumping into myself.

Well, minor jaunts aside, it looks as though all my to-ing and fro-ing to have the odd day out on the dear, old *Somerset and Dorset* and the *Weston, Clevedon and Portishead Railways*, or to go and see the premiere performance of *The Lark Ascending* at *Shirehampton Village Hall*, or making sure that I was present in *The Lamplighters Inn* to pour beer down William of Orange's doublet – never could stand monarchy – has had little effect. Heretofore, history has made its own adjustments and bounced back, but the removal of one amoral man from said history seems to have been the last thing that the otherwise hoary, old camel needed. But I'm getting ahead of myself here.

Oh, now that I've mentioned it, I must say that I thoroughly enjoyed the first performance of *The Lark Ascending*. It was played at one of the regular concerts put on by the Avonmouth and Shirehampton Choral Society. Just violin and piano – and I must say, Dear Hearts, that Marie Hall made her violin sing so beautifully. Well, Vaughan Williams was there to watch the performance, a fact which seems to be quite well known, but what most of the papers missed was that there were lots more composers there as well. Dotted all over the hall, they were. I remember seeing Edith Swepstone up the front, whilst all in a group at the side were Moeran, Parry, Bridge and Coates, all standing with Bax against the wall.

I'm so sorry, Dear Hearts, there I go rambling again. Where was I? Oh yes, breaking history. Well, there is such a thing as 'history fatigue' you know, Dear Hearts. In much the same as metal fatigue can suddenly and fatally make its appearance known when specific and previously absent periodic vibrations affect something – a ship or aeroplane, perhaps – that has otherwise stood the test of time and use without so much as a sheared bolt and the thing either sinks like a stone or shakes itself to pieces in the sky without warning. In much the same fashion, I was about to break history.

It started innocuously enough. The Captain and I wanted a holiday. Remember, Dear Hearts, that we never have a day off. Well, sort of. Actually we have a lot of holidays and days off, but we use these anomalies in time to pop us back just after we left, which is pretty much the same thing. This is why people in Pill always look a lot older than their chronological age. It's because most of them are, in fact, far, far older. I mean we can't any of us be sure, but old Marzo Plod from down near Yatton way is said to be nearly five hundred years old. What's more, it could be true. The trouble is that we all lose track of all the time spent in various diversions and all just stick with whatever we think we were at the last birthday. Makes it all so much easier.

For example, some of the local lads that were rather worried about their upcoming GCSE exams decided to pop forward in time for a week or so the night before so as to find out what was on the exam paper and to then get at least some revision done. Well, a couple of weeks turned into several adventure-packed years, as they do. They were almost stopped from sitting the exam the next day because they all had full beards and were a clear foot taller than the other pupils. Luckily for them, the senior invigilator had been in on a few of their adventures and wangled it somehow. They still all failed. Too many adventures and still not enough – or indeed any – revision, I'm afraid. Still, by that time they all had plenty of treasure buried close handy for a rainy thirty years or so.

But I'm getting side-tracked again, aren't I, Dear Hearts? Deliberately so probably. I think that I'd better just tell you it like it was. Yes, the Captain and I wanted a holiday on Brindle Holm in our favourite part of the late 18th century, but that was starting to become quite difficult. We'd pretty much block-booked our rooms in *The Grimalkin* throughout the period, though we were very careful never to meet ourselves. Often, the Landlord would say goodbye to us in the four ale bar, then wander through to the snug to say hello to us. At one point we had to stay in different rooms than usual because we were already staying in our usual ones. I think that the Captain's slide rule must have been a bit sticky that day. Mealtimes were somewhat difficult to organise I seem to remember. Hence we decided to check out a different era.

Now, the Captain, apart from collecting fossils and reading those exemplary Hal Jons westerns, is an avid military historian and was keen to stay on Brindle Holm during WW2. The plan was that we'd use the island as a base for him to get a look at the various Q weapons being tested on Brean Down and Birnbeck, and even to visit the old Starfish site a bit further along the Mendips.

What starfish were doing inland is anyone's guess, but he insists that they were there. And that the Germans used to bomb them. Well, I don't call that very fair. Talking of which, this feeling of a need to attack harmless things in times of war seems to have no rhyme nor reason to it. I mean, I remember staying in a very pleasant bed and breakfast house in Poole Harbour many years ago. Why on earth the Japanese, of all people, had decided to attack it back in 1941 is beyond comprehension. Sleepy little place, don't you know, Dear Hearts. And why on earth this should have prompted the Americans to come in on our side, I really can't think. But I digress.

Anyway, back to these Q weapons. The captain's going to write a book about them and thought that the best way to do this wasn't through lots of stuffy, old research in boring, old libraries, but by going and having a gander. How sensible – now that's what I call primary research.

I, meanwhile, was going to catch up with a spot of knitting for several ships-worth of notorious pirates and test the quality of the Milk Stout. Oh yes, Dear Hearts, I forgot to mention that I was now working part-time for Pill Brewery, testing their beers for them. Well, just the Milk Stout, to be honest, but, because I'm one of the major shareholders, no-one has yet plucked up the courage to suggest that I should test any of the others, excellent though they are, but, when all's said and done, I know what I like. Though I'm not too sure that 'testing' quite covers everything I do on tasting duties. I mean, the brewery gets the end of evening singsongs and knees-ups gratis.

Anyway, we broke open a new slide rule, just to be on the safe side, even though there was plenty of juice left in the old one. We didn't want to end up in the Black Sea again. We'd ended up there by mistake on one occasion. The mistake wasn't wasted, though, because whilst we were there we bought another ferry. It was the dead spit of our boat, *Margaret*, and we'd taken an instant liking to it. Despite not speaking the lingo, we'd waved a wad of Pill Pounds at the owner and had managed to make ourselves understood by talking more loudly than usual. We brought the ferry boat back to Pill and so we can now proudly boast that our customers get to ride on a rather euphonious Black Sea taxi, when *Margaret*, our usual Ferry is being overhauled.

Just an aside, Dear Hearts. As mentioned a couple of times already, since the last set of adventures, I've learned an interesting trick from a stranger that I'd got chatting to in the snug of *The Grimalkin*, one evening. Well, not a stranger any longer, but none other than the Oswald Bastable I mentioned in passing back in the first chapter. The upshot is that I no longer need the time gates, or whatever they're called, to move between different places and times, but have *internalised* it all. So, all I need to do now is to twist my mind, just so – there is a trick, or a knack to it, just like with juggling – and I pop up wherever and wherever it is that I want. The first hundred or so attempts were very messy failures, with my balls, metaphorically speaking of course, Dear Hearts, ending up scattered all over the place.

Then came the day that it suddenly worked – a bit like finally seeing a *Magic Eye* picture, or so I've been told; I just go all cross-eyed and get a migraine if I try. Well, I hadn't expected it to work, so I'd been idly thinking of going to the Moon – that was probably in my mind because I'd just been reading a few pages of *Easy Journey To Other Planets*, yet another that in a long line of useless charity shop books, just like that silly, old book on Soft Systems Methodology. Complete rubbish. I don't know why I bother to buy them and read them. And isn't it just so obvious that the CATWOEs – I didn't like the sound of those, I can tell you – are all developed so as to match what the client wants to hear despite pretending to objectivity? Well, it doesn't do, I suppose, to contradict the person who has the ability to deny payment, Dear Hearts, but I'm all for truth. Really.

What's that, Dear Hearts? You're not interested in these silly, old CATWOEs, whatever they are, and what was it like on the Moon? Well, I'm glad that you asked.

Yes, there I was, sitting in the snug one moment and then the next, all of a sudden, there I was surrounded by dust and rocks in a grey wilderness. Horrible, desolate place; no atmosphere at all. I thought myself back to the snug somewhat sharpish, I can tell you, though I grabbed hold of a close-handy American flag first. Where that's got to will worry them at some point I would imagine. So there we have it, Tabitha Miggins, first cat on the Moon, Dear Hearts. Now back to the story.

The Captain hadn't yet got the hang of this new method of getting from one place and time to another. Besides, only small objects and the clothes you wear can be moved with you. Even if the Captain had the knack of it, we'd never have got the Ferry there and we needed it to take various home comforts, including our instruments, of course.

Talking of which, I'd recently learned a new shanty, *The Corncrake*, written by my old friend, Nobby Dye. Whitebeard is rather fond of that one because it's all about a ship that he'd once set light to – might have been successful too, if it had been built of wood. He never has quite got the hang of steamships. Still, many's the time we've accompanied Nutter's wonderfully-authentic, cracked and out-of-tune voice with euphonium and accordion at *The Duke* – and, if he's there, Whitebeard plays along on triangle. We generally have to pay for the resulting damage.

Further Adventures of Tabitha Miggins...

Talking of Whitebeard, I remember that the last time I saw him he was complaining that it isn't fair that it should be the hair that appeared last that should be the first to go white – you'd think that, logically, it should be the hair on your head that's been there years longer that goes white first. Well, I've known stranger things; I told him all about one of my ex-Colonial Companion colleagues, a big, bruising, black tom – father of generations of kittens – who had a bad fright and turned suddenly ginger overnight. Never looked at another female cat again.

Well, that aside, we did the usual nautical piggery jokery in the Channel and popped up just short of Brindlesea. The harbour seemed very subdued and the few people around stared at us closely. Still, we didn't really pay too much attention. Whitebeard's ship was tied up and I rather looked forward to having a chinwag when we met up. Funny that he should be here at the same *different* time as us. Anyway, we headed into *The Grimalkin* and were heartily greeted by the same landlord that we knew from the late 18th century.

"Well, hello! Mighty glad I am to see you two. You'll soon put things to rights, won't you Tabitha?"

After my initial surprise, I said happily, "Not half, we'll have the usuals."

This didn't seem to be quite what he'd meant by putting things to rights.

"Ah, a shame and no mistake, but your usuals is one thing that you can't have. We've not had any deliveries since them Nasties arrived. Well, we sees the deliveries on the harbour all right, but we never gets to see the beer. Off to their boat, I reckon it all goes, only it's us publicans that Pill Brewery invoices all the same."

"What nasties?" I asked, wondering whether some monsters or other had broken through from some nightmare realm or other.

"Them Nasties," the Landlord replied as the door was banged open and a group of armed sailors appeared, all pointing guns at us.

"You are all under arrest," bawled the officer in near immaculate English, but with a hint of an accent.

The uniforms said it all, though. Not nasties but Nazis. The Kriegsmarine was in charge of Brindle Holm.

"I'll see you later for a bit of a chat," murmured the Landlord as we were manhandled – well, cathandled in my case, of course, Dear Hearts – out through the door.

The Captain put up a bit of a fight and got put out of commission by a nasty whack on the head from the chief Nazi's pistol. Well, that wasn't a nice thing to do – hang on a second, wasn't that Whitebeard's heavy, woollen breeches that he was wearing. I say, the chap had been at Whitebeard's personal possessions by the look of it. I bet that he'd regret that when Whitebeard got to hear of it. In fact, I wondered where Whitebeard and his crew were. Their boat was here but there was no sign of them. Oh well, I guessed that I would find out in due course.

The Captain was put onto a ramshackle bed in the gunpowder house on the quay, which was now being used as a cell by the look of things. Using this as some sort of prison was sensible I suppose because it did have the thickest walls of any building on the island. I was bundled into the next cell with no ceremony whatsoever and, of all things, even had my knitting bag confiscated by the chief Nazi. I'll just wait until no-one's looking, I thought, and then I'll think myself out of the cell to have a bit of a chat with the landlord and pick up my knitting bag on the way. An idle though meandered through my mind, which concerned whether Brindle Holm was neutral territory or not. I mean, it wasn't part of the British Isles, even if it was theoretically in British territorial waters. If neutral, then I would say that the current occupation was well and truly *Against The Rules*.

Anyway, I let my mind twist just so and, once I'd picked up my knitting bag from inside the padlocked room in which it had been deposited – and just don't ask me how I knew where to look for it – I just knew, that's all – I twisted my mind again in a slightly different way and appeared much later that same day in the now closed *Grimalkin*, where the landlord was waiting for me. Usually, *The Grimalkin* would just be coming to life at this time in the evening, but somehow I'd just known that there would be a curfew and the public houses would be closed at ten.

Well, whether the Germans knew it or not, they certainly knew how to go about fomenting revolution, I'll say that for them. Keep Brindleholmians away from their beer for more than two nights running and my guess is that there would be no need for any sort of intervention on my part. Except that that would lead to needless bloodshed on the part of the islanders. No guns on Brindle Holm, except for those carried by the Germans, the Landlord told me amongst other things, which I'm just about to tell you about.

Further Adventures of Tabitha Miggins...

Yes, we had that nice, little chat and I learned a lot of things about the Nazi Kapitän, none of them particularly nice. A complete fanatic he was and, according to the landlord, more like Hitler than der Führer himself. He had commandeered the best room in the inn, which just happened to be the one that Whitebeard had only just booked into, and had made free with his possessions, including lots of garments that I'd made especially for my friend. Well, there was a black mark against him for a start.

His men were evidently a decent enough bunch but seemed somewhat frightened of their Kapitän and were quick to do his bidding in case he took one of his frequent tantrums out on them. Indeed, whilst the chief Nazi lorded it from Whitebeard's room, his men either roughed it in one of the warehouses on the quay or slept aboard their Schnellboot. Indeed, the Nazi sounded like one of those dangerous people, not all being men by any means, that live inside an ideology that puts them at the top of the tree and puts everyone else, even their families and closest allies, somewhere lower down the order, no matter what the ideology states in terms of equality.

The Landlord told me that the Kapitän didn't even know the names of the men under his command and instead referred to them by the Roman numerals that he had ordered them to sew onto their lapels. For example, The Nazi Kapitän referred to the one with the Roman numeral "V" on his uniform as "Funf". The Brindleholmians at least dignified his profession and called him 'Sailor V'. Well, that's life, I suppose, Dear Hearts. Still, people should have names, not numbers, is what I say but, thinking about it, I wonder where that leaves Fauré?

But that's enough of idle musing, Dear Hearts.

So, the Nazi was Kapitän of a Schnellboot and he and his crew had taken over Brindle Holm the night before. That much had become clear, but there were still so many questions to ask. For a start, where was Whitebeard and did he know that his room and possessions had been stolen by the Schnellboot Kapitän? And how on earth had a boatful of German sailors come to find Brindle Holm in the first place?

What's that, Dear Hearts? What's a Schnellboot when it's at home? Well, they tend to be called E Boats over here but I always like to call things by their real names. For one thing it keeps the dimwits guessing, don't you know. Well, 'Schnell' means 'fast' and you should have guessed by now that 'boot' is German for 'boat', which explains why I put the boot in.

Anyway, back to the story. As for Whitebeard and his crew, the Landlord told me they had all been in a serious state of inebriation in *The Grimalkin* the previous evening when the Germans had burst in at each door simultaneously and taken them by surprise. A few bursts of Schmeisser fire into the walls above their heads had convinced those that were still awake and paying attention that resistance was not really an option. Even Whitebeard went quietly. This was the first that anyone knew that the management had changed on Brindle Holm.

It's funny how such a bloodthirsty group of people should know exactly when not to fight. I suppose that pirates are used to sizing things up and only having a go when things are in their favour. Well, that or when they just fancy a fight no matter what the odds. They were all now under lock and key in some dreadful, squat, concrete storehouses that certainly hadn't been there in the eighteenth century – so progress even comes to Brindle Holm. Talking of the eighteenth century, what on earth were Whitebeard and his crew doing here in the twentieth century in any case when they should have been nicely tucked up in seventeen something or other? Well, I'd probably find out in due course.

As for how the Schnellboot had found Brindle Holm, the Landlord didn't know, though he had a shrewd idea that it might have had something to do with a boatload of German merchant seamen that had stumbled across the island slightly in advance of the outbreak of the First World War after they had accidentally sailed through one of the time gates in a bit of a rush to get out of Avonmouth docks and British waters when it became clear that war was about to be declared.

Well, they'd pulled in at Brindlesea, mainly because they couldn't work out where they were – I mean, not surprising really, but Brindle Holm wasn't on any of their charts. Though talking of Admiralty Charts, one of the local hobblers did his first ever work experience, whilst still at school in the 1970s, in *W. F. Price*, the Admiralty Chart Correcting Agency – up past the Post Office in Gloucester Road in Avonmouth it was, back in those days. Well, there'd always been a rumour around Pill that charts existed that included Brindle Holm and other magical locations along with all the time gates, but no-one had ever been able to substantiate it. Well, what with being an inquisitive fifteen-year-old at that point, this lad had stumbled on a hidden safe one lunchtime when everyone else had gone off to the *Royal*

Hotel for the usual Friday liquid lunch. Now, he already knew about the safe where all the money was kept overnight, but he'd become very curious about the contents of the 'other' safe that he'd very obviously not been told about. Why it is that adults think that children don't know exactly what it is that they have deliberately not told them, I just don't know. Children are naturally inquisitive, or at least they were back in the days when they were encouraged to use their brains.

Well, chucking out time was 2.30 in those days so he knew that he had a good hour to try to crack the safe before anyone would even think of coming back to work. It took him about three minutes, what with it being a deadlock type and the key being in the main safe, which he'd already cracked and riffled through on day one. Inside there was a chart with lots of locations marked up on it. Someone there was obviously in the know and by the look of it must have been scanning all the charts that came in from ships visiting Avonmouth Docks for correction and transcribing any interestingly hand-added anomalies across.

Well, the boy didn't think it safe that someone not from one of the magical places should know too much and he'd decided to help safeguard Brindle Holm and all those other places included on the map. By the time everyone returned from lunch, there was a new chart in the safe that looked in all respects to be the same as the other one, but with everything moved just enough so that it wouldn't be noticeable but certainly enough to make it completely inaccurate and harmless at the same time.

What's that, Dear Hearts? What did he do with the real one? Well, it's very well hidden is all that I'm going to say. We know how to keep secrets here in Pill. Oh dear, I do hope that I haven't said a bit too much here. I'll tell you what, Dear Hearts, shall we make this just our secret? You won't tell anyone will you? Good, I knew that I could trust you.

Anyway, I seem to be meandering again, so back to the merchantman crew. They'd evidently been a cheerful bunch and not particularly interested in fighting, so once it became obvious that the locals were friendly and not particularly at war with anyone, except smugglers from Lundy, that is, and that they were safe from both the British and German authorities they'd stayed on until hostilities had ceased and then concocted some story or other about having had their ship interned.

Of course, they'd all got to know about the time gates in their everyday lives on the island in various runs over to the mainland whenever the islanders had business over there. The Landlord didn't think that any of them would have given the secret away, but perhaps one of them was tortured into it. You never know.

So I decided, whilst supposedly locked in my cell, to head back in time to find out if there was any connection between the German sailors that hid themselves here and the current Nazi infestation. I thought that a spot of whizzing around in inter-war Germany and doing a spot of cloak and dagger work might help me to put together the whole story. In any case, it would give me something to do whilst I thought of how to sort out the current problem. I already had the glimmerings of a plan based on seeing the Nazi wearing Whitebeard's special breeches, but I wanted to be sure that my currently vague idea wouldn't have any serious repercussions. It was also a little drastic, so I wanted to see if there were any alternatives. I mean, it's not in my nature to be vindictive just for the sake of it.

Although I could pretty much come and go as I pleased and pop myself back a split-second after I'd left it wouldn't do to be spotted somewhere, when I was supposed to be locked up nice and safely, would it? So, the first thing I did was to pop off to some cover above the village so that I could see the Germans' comings and goings from *The Grimalkin* and the various harbourside buildings that they'd commandeered.

I saw the Nazi captain leave the public house and head off to the Schnellboot to shout at some of his crew so I thought myself into his room to have a quick look at his papers. What with the neat, Teutonic mind, they'll be in Whitebeard's bureau, I'd guess; and I'd be right – here they are. Kapitän Heinrich Wilhelm Braun, born August 1919. Well, if his father was one of those seamen from WW1 he didn't waste much time starting a family once he got home, that's all that I can say, Dear Hearts.

Hm, photograph of Mutti complete with inscription, "Unterscheiden Sie sich für die Ehre deines geliebten Führer und Vaterland, mit aller Liebe von Ihrem liebste Mutter, Gertrud." A little formal, perhaps, but then what would I know about such things? Hm, no photo of his father. That would be too easy, I suppose. Oh well, let's go and ask the Landlord if he remembers the names of the German seamen.

Further Adventures of Tabitha Miggins...

    The Landlord confirmed that one of the seamen, a quiet, likable chap, had been called Braun and further informed me that the ship's name was *Mathilda*, a coastal trader out from Hamburg. He also gave me the date that they'd left Brindle Holm and headed through the time gate, so I headed back to post-war Hamburg to find out what happened next.
    Well, when the boat arrived in dock later that same day the crew was given a good welcome based on their supposed incarceration in a British prison camp since the first day of war. Quite how they'd got through the allied naval blockade never was sensibly explained. Well, of course I know that they'd used the time gate to arrive just offshore here. In fact, the crew didn't know anything of the blockade but their obvious astonishment on hearing about how impossible it should have been to get through was taken merely as supreme confidence in their superior seamanship and so they were feted as heroes, this at a time when Germany was in desperate need of something to celebrate. It has to be said that they looked a lot better fed than their countrymen but that didn't stop them from getting a good meal inside them PDQ.
    I managed to spot the right chap almost immediately because he was the living spit of his loony son – and there, unless I was very much mistaken, was Gertrud, working as a waitress in the dock canteen and currently waiting on the crew. Ah, yes, there seems to be some sort of attraction going on between those two. Funny how these things work, evidently. I mean, I've never been tainted with any sort of romance – too sensible, me – but Lavinia seems to know all about these things.
    Luckily there were plenty of cats about in the docks and my presence went unnoticed. I've always found that a spot of seemingly idle knitting, interspersed with bouts of determined cleaning behind the ears is a good way to blend into the background and allay any sort of suspicion.
    Well, quite how I found out what I did would make very boring reading, so I'll just give you the gist of what my spying on the Braun family once a year or so over the next twenty years brought to light. And I think that it was quite good going based on the fact that I was incarcerated in a cell overnight the whole time, don't you, Dear Hearts? What's that, you'll let me know when I've told you? Oh yes, I haven't told you yet, have I? I don't know. My mind must be wandering a bit, I think.

Further Adventures of Tabitha Miggins...

Well, here we go. As for doing things quickly, well a week later Wilhelm and Gurtrud were married. Perhaps it was something to do with the fact that Gertrud worked in a canteen and that Wilhelm had just worked out how little food there was in post-war Germany. And, yes, Heinrich was born just ten months later. Well, what with very little to eat and not much for sailors to do, what with the ongoing blockade, this probably wasn't too surprising after all.

Well, Wilhelm remained as a merchantman for a few more years, once the Treaty of Versailles allowed some sort of merchant fleet to exist again, that is, whilst Heinrich grew up with Gertrud. Perhaps this is why mother and son turned out the way they did. Whilst the father was away for much of the time, disconnected by both job and distance from what was going on inside Germany, both mother and son began to turn by degrees into jolly good Arians. Well, what else were they going to do?

As soon as he was old enough Heinrich joined the Grossdeutsche Jugendbewegung, where he learned to tie knots and despise anything tarred with the word 'Juden'. In 1933, on the movement's inception, he joined the Hitlerjugend and did rather well for himself, what with nature having bestowed blond hair and blue eyes on him, taking all Party messages as gospel, not that that particular word would have had any currency at that point in Germany's history, of course, Dear Hearts.

I always think that the British should think themselves lucky that nothing of this sort ever took off seriously in this country because indoctrination is something that is very easy to do with the young and impressionable. How wonderful that our own youth institutions should always have concentrated on inculcating self-loathing, mediocrity and knowing your place.

On the other hand, many of our own bright and beautiful were taken in by the glitz and glitter of the Third Reich. I mean, I just happened to be there, for some reason or other that I forget for the moment, when that silly Utility Mitford gel shot herself in the head, and all because der Führer didn't laugh at her joke about the invasion of Czechoslovakia having been a goosestep in the Reich direction.

Do you know, Dear Hearts, she couldn't even shoot herself properly? No, she missed first go and shot Himmler in the nose. I later heard that, despite the pain involved in getting the bullet out, he still held a soft spot for her for years afterwards. Funny things, men.

Still, they all seemed such funny people, those Nazis. Old Mad-Alf, as we used to call Herr Hitler, had only ever been invited to one ball, which I thought very sad and not at all good for his societal development. Well, this was according to something Lavinia once told me, not that I was really listening. I mean, what on earth was he doing at the Albert Hall when he should have been at some Rally or Putsch or some such? She went on to say something about Goering preferring smaller gatherings, as did Himmler – well, it's so much more intimate, isn't it? – not that they were invited to many more than old Mad-Alf from what I remember. I did feel sorry for poor, old Goebbels, though – I mean furballs are so tiresome, don't you know, what with all that dry retching? Sorry, Dear Hearts, I'm getting away from the point again, aren't I?

But back to Heinrich and Gertrud. Just remember, before you cast blame, that if you were there, you would have believed in the Nazi dream as well. It takes a very special person to think critically about what they're told – especially when the dream is so real – and to look behind all the panoply and splendour to see what's really there. It's much easier to just believe. Especially when those that do question tend to suddenly disappear in the middle of the night.

Anyway, I'm wandering again. Where was I? Oh yes, Wilhelm eventually left the merchant fleet in 1931 and started up a quite humble business, mending and making parts for motor bikes and bicycles. He was inordinately proud of his first lathe, I remember. He'd saved most of his pay, from the small amount that he'd not sent back to his wife and child, in order to buy it and it certainly helped to win him lots of trade in the area. I couldn't help thinking what a nice man he was; quiet and unassuming, with very simple tastes and I couldn't quite believe the fanatic his child was to turn into.

Anyway, I visited once a year or so just to keep tabs and then rather more so once war had started just to see what happened. Something told me that the period immediately prior to the Schnellboot appearing at Brindle Holm was probably the time to spend a little more time in attendance. Funny how an elderly tabby cat with accompanying knitting motif still seems to fade into the background. I was starting to suspect that my presence would make someone or other suspicious, but no. Besides, there are a lot more places to clean properly than just behind the Urals.

Further Adventures of Tabitha Miggins...

Well, in 1938, Willhelm joined the Kriegsmarine and after a year or so of intensive training and some conspicuous bravery on one patrol out into the English Channel in late 1941 he suddenly found himself decorated and fast-tracked to Kapitän of his own Schnell Boot. His father was very proud of his son's achievements, but was also very worried for his safety. Anyway, after being decorated and promoted Heinrich was given a week's shore leave at which point Wilhelm decided to let his son in on the secret of Brindle Holm so that, if necessary, he could hide out the war in safety. He didn't want his wife to know, so he suggested a walk in the local park.

Well, I knew the topology of the district by now and made sure that I was there ahead of them and already a part of the general view, so to speak. There was only one bench and I was sure that Wilhelm would choose to sit before speaking to his son. I was right and as they sat together at the bench, all they would have been able to see in the close vicinity was an elderly tabby cat playing its bangolorum, as the saying goes. I knew that this must be it, so my strenuous licking was all sham, otherwise I would never have been able to hear anything over the slurping sound.

I have to say that Wilhelm completely misinterpreted the enthusiasm with which his son took the news of Brindle Holm and the time gate. Well, son thanked father effusively and then asked for some time on his own with his mother so as to prepare her for possibly a long absence. Father, of course, thought that son was going to disappear for the duration, but of course I knew better and wanted to find out what it was that he told his mother.

When Heinrich arrived home a few minutes later there was an elderly tabby cat taking in the last of the afternoon sun and cleaning residual amounts of wool somewhat lazily out of various paws in the garden just outside the open kitchen window.

Well, I have to say that Heinrich didn't have a good word to say for his father and called him a coward of the first water. There was even talk of having him arrested by the authorities. Gertrud, however, said that she would deal with it. Son and mother looked hard into each-other's eyes and seemed to understand each other. I didn't think that anything good was about to happen to poor, old Wilhelm on his return. Well, the son did say goodbye to his mother and did explain that he might be gone for a while, but the inference was clear that he was going to tell his superiors about Brindle Holm for the good of Führer and Fatherland.

Well, I knew what happened next in terms of the son, because he was currently holding me prisoner in the cell on Brindle Holm, or so he thought, but what of his father and mother. Well, that would have to wait because all of this to-ing and fro-ing had left me somewhat esurient. This is slightly odd, I know, but even though I did all my visits in the same night, from my point of view, I always felt the need to get sufficient sustenance each time I visited. Well, what can you expect? It may all have happened overnight, but it took about three weeks altogether.

And talking of food, it has to be said that I could find hardly anything suitable to eat in my various jaunts back to 1930's Germany thanks to the country's focus being on armaments and consumer goods instead of food. A funny combination that, I always thought. I mean, what were they expecting to do when the food ran out and most of the consumer goods became useless? Drop fridges on us, I suppose. In any case, how on earth, when it came to my own need for nutrition, was I expected to eat? I never could stand pickled cabbage and as for that awful rye bread, well, the least said the better. In fact, all I can say is that, as the 1930s progressed, the food in pre-war Germany went from brat to wurst. Oh, you didn't laugh. Don't blame you on reflection, Dear Hearts.

Anyway, as the war got underway I had to be a bit more careful in my visits thanks to the upshot of even worse food shortages. I mean, there was that restaurant that always seemed to be so full. The one that had a sign in the window saying, "Wir servieren Katzen." Well, I only just escaped that one with fur intact by the tip of my whisker, even with my ability to move through time and space at the turn of a thought. It looks as though my translation skills were not quite up to scratch that particular day, Dear Hearts.

Anyway, why all this talk about food suddenly, you may well ask, Dear Hearts? Well it's because of what happened as soon as the unnatural boy had told his equally unnatural mother about his father's real war experience, or lack of one, that food became of a certain importance. As soon as Gertrud found out that her husband was a coward, as she also put it, and not fit to be a member of the most glorious Reich ever to be put upon this earth by the most wonderful man, der Führer, she decided to poison him and to devote herself to the Party.

Heinrich had gone back to base by the time that her plans had fully matured the following day. Quick to make up her mind and act was dear, old Gertrud. Decisive and barking mad, if you ask me. I don't know what poor, old Wilhelm had seen in her. Well, what with meeting and being married and all within a couple of weeks, probably not a lot when all is said and done. Marry in haste, repent at leisure and all that, don't you know, Dear Hearts? That and die in agony as things turned out.

Well, her plan was to make Wilhelm a special meal and to add a huge dollop of poison. Somehow she got together the ingredients for his favourite meal. Well, what with rationing it was easier than it might have been because his favourite food was borscht. Lucky that, because about the only thing in any sort of plentiful supply was beetroot. The fact that borscht is a dark, red colour also covered up the fact that the special ingredient was arsenic.

But isn't arsenic colourless – or at least white – so why should it have been detected in any case if it was well mixed in, I hear you ask, Dear Hearts?

Good heavens, well, if you're that sharp then I think that your little brother should watch out for you. How on earth do you know so much about arsenic? Well, what you might not know is that powdered arsenic was easily bought from chemist shops back in those less over-regulated days, but so as not to be confused for sugar or salt, with all the hilarious consequences that might perpetrate, it was pigmented with iodine so that it was obvious to all not to add it liberally to food.

Well, old Gertrud played the faithful wife for all it was worth as poor, old Wilhelm went through it all. Told Herr Doktor that it was the old gastric trouble again and by the time the poor, old chap had finally shuffled off this mortal thingummy in absolute agony, three days later, there wasn't the slightest quibble about giving the death certificate. Acute gastritis with complications.

Not a nice way to go and I nearly burst my head trying to think of ways that I could alter the course of history so that Wilhelm would survive, but all of them seemed to have some flaw or another. One rather elaborate plan involved going back again to 1919 and somehow preventing him from meeting Gertrud and introducing him to someone else instead so that, if he had to have a son, that son might at least possess genes from a less mad mother.

Yes, Dear Hearts, catching at straws. All pie in the sky, of course. I mean, how on earth could I have contrived to do all that? In any case, I had a dream that night that Gertrud, instead of meeting and marrying Wilhelm, had met and married some chap called Schicklgruber and that the Nazis had won the war in any case, thanks to her taking over management and all that from a very early stage. Oh it was all so complicated.

Then, of course, I had my brainwave. If I removed the son from history so that he'd never existed, then Wilhelm could safely marry Gertrud and, without the son to tell of his past, Wilhelm would not be poisoned by his wife. So simple when you came to think of it. Now, how could I arrange for Heinrich never to have existed? Ah, yes, here was the plan, fully-formed in my mind. Again, so simple when you thought about it. And the funny thing was that I'd already thought of most of it and the last part had now slotted into place.

And to think that the Nazi in question had only himself to blame in part. He'd already stolen one pair of Whitebeard's special breeches; you know, Dear Hearts, the ones that I accidentally knitted twice. The solution to the problem, however, required that they would have to exist three times instead of only twice, something that I needed to do a spot of thinking about.

Or better still, instead of worrying my poor, old head about it, why didn't I just go ahead in time and have a quick chat with myself to see how I did it? After all, I never did quite work out how I could have knitted the same pair twice in the first place. All against The Rules, deliberately going to talk to yourself, I know, but I've generally found that rules can be sidled around if given enough forethought and a spot of lateral thinking. That or a bulldozer.

What's that, Dear Hearts? How did I suddenly know that breeches cubed would be the solution? Good question, Dear Hearts, and one that I can't answer sensibly. I just knew, that's all. A lot of life is like that. Call it intuition. Call it what you will. All I knew was that I had an interesting knitting problem on my hands. Once more unto the breeches, Dear Hearts. Well, twice if what I suspected turned out to be true.

First, though, I managed to be in the vicinity of Heinrich and his immediate superior on their first meeting after Heinrich's leave was over. Now it always amazes me that people can believe in things like magical islands with no proof whatsoever, but then it struck me that it all fitted in perfectly with the nonsensical unreality that was the made-up mythology underpinning the very notion of the Third Reich. Well, the upshot of that interview, as I dealt most convincingly with a patch of particularly matted fur, was that the loony son was given permission to take his boat and crew to make a base on Brindle Holm, create havoc in the Bristol Channel and then come back with a plan for how to further exploit the time gate.

Right, now was the time for that little chat with myself. Well, going to talk to yourself deliberately is a bit tricky, unlike bumping into yourself by accident, which happens all the time if you're not too careful. I don't intend to tell you how it's done – well, not quite yet. All I'll say is that I headed off to a certain future time in a specifically indirect way and knocked a special knock on my door so as to let myself know that I was visiting. Haven't got a clue when I organised that one with myself, Dear Hearts.

Well, I found a nice, comfortable chair waiting for me just one side of the doorway between living room and kitchen and sat myself down. I knew that the future me would be sitting in the matching chair just the other side of the door. The Rules, you see, say that you cannot deliberately go and talk to yourself face-to-face. Sloppy wording, I call that. So we sat either side of the doorway with the wall between us so that we couldn't see each other.

So, first things first. My plan was to knit the same pair of breeches three times. I'd already knitted them twice. Or, at least, Whitebeard had the same pair twice, not that I had the faintest idea how that could actually have come about because I'd only knitted them once. I wanted to know first and foremost if my plan was, theoretically speaking, a goer, or was I meowing up the wrong tree altogether?

Well, I told myself that there was nothing whatsoever wrong with the theory, but that reality might throw up a few problems along the way but not to worry about it if it did. I have a funny feeling that I was about to say something else to myself at this point but just at that moment the kettle started to whistle, so I knew that some tea would soon be forthcoming. Oh, I really hoped that there would be some nice cream cakes as well. Yes, there were – some of Crusty Gerrish's finest, by the taste of them. We pushed the trolley through the doorway to each other and did the doings before getting back down to business.

So, my future self was happy that my plan was theoretically possible. And as this particular me had already lived through this part, it must all have been satisfactory because, well, here I still was. But I thought that I'd better just ask, based on my concerns.

"I don't," I began, somewhat hesitantly, "Manage to do anything to, um, muck up history, do I?"

"No," I reassured myself, "Everything works out well, so don't worry."

Well, my plan had legs and would not hurt history, so those were my main worries assuaged. So now came the question about the mechanics of the thing. I mean, how on earth is it possible to knit the same thing three times?

Well, I told myself that my curiosity was well-founded and that, as I'd guessed, although Whitebeard currently possessed the same pair of breeches twice, I'd as yet only knitted them once. Yes, I know that I'd unpicked them and started again, if you remember, Dear Hearts, once I'd seen the nice, herringbone pattern that I'd come up with for the first pair, but that didn't count. So I would have to go and knit them again just so that the current reality had caught up with events. I could then go and knit them for the third time when the time came.

"So, how do I knit them the first time?" I asked.

"Well," I replied to myself, "You have to go outside of space and time to do it."

I was a little non-plussed by this.

"How on earth do I do that, then?" I asked. "I mean; I haven't got a clue how to. I know how to move *in* space and time, but to go outside?"

"Nonsense, you do it all the time."

"No I don't...oh, yes I do."

Yes, it all suddenly made sense. Of course, it had to be done on Brindle Holm. But when?

Well, I told myself that I would have to go to the top of Brindle Hill on the 31st February – that particular date had only ever happened once, and that thanks to a rather interesting anomaly during changeover from the old Sandy calendar to the Gregorian one. All I had to do was to think myself there by twisting my mind, just so, and I'd appear in the right place. I could then intersect somehow with the earlier version of me knitting the second pair in the snug at *The Duke* all those years ago. Not a clue how it was to be done, but that it would happen was a given.

I'm afraid I sniggered rather a lot when I went on to tell myself about how I'd done my best to annoy Heinrich before dealing with him. Oh dear, so I could be vindictive after all. But, Dear Hearts, what an audacious plan I'd hatched.

So, as regards the original pair of breeches, I headed off to Brindle Hill on the 31st February, did what I had to do and dropped them back at *The Grimalkin* ready for Whitebeard to pick up just before I'd knitted the second pair. So, at least current reality was up-to-date as regards the right number of breeches in both theory and fact. Lovely herringbone pattern, too.

What's that, Dear Hearts, how exactly was it done? Oh, I'm so glad that you're interested. Here's how:

Row 1: *Ssk, dropping only the first stitch off your needle,* rep from * to last st, k.
Row 2: *P2tog, dropping only the first stitch off your needle,* rep from * to last st, p.
Repeat rows 1 and 2 until required width is reached.

Now, having already watched the comings and goings to and from my cell from the hill, I knew when Heinrich was going to come and question me so I made some preparations first. Some were quite complicated and took rather a lot of time, but I can't be bothered to explain every little thing, otherwise the jolly, old narrative will be thoroughly confusing and will lose rather a lot of pep, Dear Hearts. All I'm going to say is that I thought I'd give him the run-around before wiping him out of history. Besides, I already knew that I did.

It was morning when, sitting in the one and only chair, deliberately not doing any knitting, I heard the key turn in the lock. The Kapitän covered me with his pistol as he entered, dragging a second chair from outside. He placed it opposite mine and, still brandishing the pistol, sat down debonairly. He was wearing a thick, white, navy-issue jumper along with Whitebeard's knitted breeches.

"My name is Kapitän Braun, Kriegsmarine," the loony began, "And I am curious about two things. Firstly, why you and your companion appeared so soon after myself and my crew. Did you know we were here or was it pure accident? If the latter, then it was quite an unlucky accident for you both. Secondly, why do I get the distinct feeling that I know you from somewhere? You are very familiar, but I cannot quite put my finger on why this should be so."

There was almost a cat joke in there, I couldn't help but notice – you know, the 'familiar' one – but I don't suppose for one moment that it was deliberate. Well, I thought that I'd answer bits of his question in my own way, but I was, I have to admit, first and foremost, curious about the gun that the loony was pointing at me. It was quite an odd shape, I thought.

"I'll certainly answer your questions," I said, "But first, could you tell me what sort of gun that is?"

He gave me a look that said that he was willing to humour the silly, old biddy for a bit.

"It is a Mauser," he said.

Good heavens, I thought. He must be a jolly good shot, though I'd just get a cat myself. I mulled over this for a second or two, just whilst I was finalising my plan of attack, to be honest, and decided to start off quite normally.

"Well, the good Captain and myself were just coming here for a holiday, don't you know? Didn't have the slightest clue that the island was under new ownership and all that."

The Nazi smiled a little less nicely at this point.

"Well, a holiday is something that you will not be getting. Once your companion has woken up he'll be put in one of the work groups along with the islanders and those awful, uncouth sailors from that antiquated ship. We'll find something to keep you and the rest of the females occupied as well, so don't you worry. I noticed that you had a knitting bag. My glorious Führer is very keen on reintroducing the Cimbrian art of knitting, so you are likely to find yourself busy teaching this mystic art to our young."

Well, that sounded almost like fun, but I didn't like the sound of what the Captain would be forced to do.

"What will the work groups be doing?" I asked.

"Building Schnellboot and submarine pens to begin with. Those that survive will be sent back to the Fatherland to work for the furtherment of der Führer and our glorious Reich."

Well, I thought that it was time to introduce a note of uncertainty into his mind.

"Well, good luck on that score," I said, "Because you'll need it. Yes, to answer your second question, you do know me. Or at least, you have seen quite a lot of me over the whole of your life. If you think hard, you'll know me to be very clean living too."

He started to goggle at me a bit here. I mean, was I completely mad? I thought that it was time to tell him a little bit about himself and his family. Now I didn't want to let old Mr Jinx out of the bag completely yet, so to speak – or in the current circs perhaps that should be Fritz, Dear Hearts – but to give him just enough to perhaps start to ask himself some questions.

"I'm here," I said carefully, "Because of your father, Wilhelm. I'm here to make sure that he doesn't tell you about this island's existence."

The goggling increased. Perhaps because I'd mentioned his father by name, or perhaps because I had the air of just having tuned from interrogated to interrogator. There are subtle ways to tell when you've just lost the advantage and my mention of Wilhelm had caused just that. Or it might have been that he had just noticed that I wasn't wearing the same outfit as I had when he'd thrown me into the cell last night. I didn't ask quite which, so I can't tell you, I'm afraid, Dear Hearts.

He was, however, quick to assert himself again.

"So you knew my father. A worthless man in all respects. Luckily I take after my mother. But you make no sense. I already know the secret of this island. He has already told me. How do you think that you can you stop what has already happened?"

"There are ways," I said, smiling. "Some more pleasant than others."

A hardness came into his eyes and the gun levelled at me.

"I don't think that I can be bothered to listen to you. I don't know how you know my worthless father's name or what you think that you are talking about. Why don't I just kill you and have done with it?"

Well, I was glad that he'd brought up the topic of death.

"Do you know," I said, "If you want me to cower and beg for mercy, I'm afraid you'll stay wanting. Death holds no fear for me. In fact, I've died quite a few times already, I'll have you know."

The goggling theme returned at this, again whether he was surprised at my fearless stance or was wondering what on earth I was talking about I can't tell you. Or perhaps he'd just noticed that I was propped up against several very comfortable cushions that hadn't been there a few seconds earlier. Well, I'd used the millisecond that he'd blinked just now to nip off and start doing a few things. Anyway, whatever the reason, I wasn't going to let him get a word in edgeways at this precise moment.

"There are lots of ways to die," I continued, "You can die bravely, or you can die cowering like a cowardy-custard, or you can die in agony like your own father, poisoned by his unnatural wife – don't be so surprised that I know – or you can die in such a stupid way that people in the future will smirk or snigger when they hear your name. You, I'm afraid, are set for a stupid and quite horrendous death but because of the nature of your death, no-one will even know you existed, Fritz – oh, I'm sorry, may I call you Fritz?"

His mouth, which had been working a bit, though without any sensible sounds forthcoming, suddenly started to work again.

"No, you cannot call me Fritz," he shouted, a few flecks of froth starting to appear at the edges.

"Why not?" I asked, all innocence and as if I didn't know his name and life story intimately.

"Because my name is Heinrich," he screamed.

"But Fritz is a much nicer name. Oh, well, never mind. Still, as I was saying, Heinie..."

"Don't call me Heinie! My name is not Heinie, it's Heinrich, you half-witted moggie."

"Oh, really? What a funny surname – and what does the "U" stand for?"

He was starting to look extremely dangerous at this point so I carried on fairly quickly.

"As I was saying, Heinrich, your death will be stupid. Because you are stupid. Fanaticism makes you stupid. Your nemesis is in my knitting bag."

"Well, your knitting bag is not here," he said, smiling malevolently and casting his gaze around the room to show exactly how empty it was.

In fact, he looked away just long enough for me to carry on with some of those things that I'd prepared.

"Are you sure I don't have my knitting bag?" I said as his gaze returned to me. "So what's this?"

"How did you get that bag in here? What trickery is this? I took that bag away from you myself."

He grabbed the bag from me and looked inside.

"Nemesis? It's just a pair of breeches, just like these ones that I found in my room at the inn."

Yes, Dear Hearts, I'd just collected these from Whitebeard's room on board *The Queen Bee's Revenge*. The Nazi suddenly became aware, as he looked up from studying the contents of the bag and holding the breeches in his hand, that I was now wearing a different hat and that the previously dull, grey curtains suddenly sported a cheerful, floral pattern. I didn't let him spend too long on this, though.

"Oh, perhaps I meant this knitting bag, then," I said, nodding to a second bag on the floor at my feet.

"What is going on here?" he screamed in a rage.

He grabbed at the bag and looked inside.

"It's another pair, exactly the same – ah, and a pair of knitting needles. So, you were intending to attack me with a pair of knitting needles, were you? Did you really think that that would work?" He looked up and saw that I was now knitting from yet another knitting bag. Luckily, although I only have one *special* knitting bag, I do have a few spares just in case. I can't be sure that he picked up all the subtle nuances, but surely he couldn't have missed the fact that the drab cell was now neatly wallpapered.

Well, he was in such an apoplectic rage at this point, borne of confusion and, perhaps, the beginnings of self-doubt, that he just sat there – he was even beyond mindless violence against my poor, little self. Which, of course I'd already told myself would be the case. So I stopped knitting, settled the half-finished scarf on my knees and looked him straight in the eye.

"Fritz," I started, "And I don't give a badger's cuss – not even one of Clarence's most inventive ones – what your name is because you are a nothing, or at least, will be in a few moments. You spoke more truly than you knew when you said that those breeches were the same as the ones you are wearing. They are, in fact, exactly the same pair. Have you noticed that slight smell of burning..?"

He glanced to one side, sniffing, as I paused briefly there for reasons that may become logically clear in a moment, before continuing. By the time that he looked back I'd been and gone and returned again.

"Well, that's the start of what would in the normal course of events have been a quite spectacular explosion. I always thought that putting the second pair of breeches in your lap whilst you looked inside the second bag was a grave mistake, but on your legs be it, I thought."

The pathetic Nazi merely goggled at me – possibly because my hat had changed again during the brief pause when I'd suddenly realised what I'd forgotten to do half way through my speech and had nipped off to put it right.

Of course, I'd gone and added a timer fuse to Whitebeard's second pair otherwise they would have blown up just a few seconds after they were brought in contact together with the original pair. And I didn't want that to happen because I intended to be rather more malicious that that.

He had probably spotted the raincoat too. Well, I wasn't quite sure how messy things would get in here. Anyway, where was I, Dear Hearts? Oh yes, Nazi-baiting. Baiting the master race.

"Well, Fritz," I began again, "That third pair that you have just dropped, goggle-eyed, on top of the other pair is also exactly the same pair. Breeches cubed. Do you know what that means?"

Well, of course he didn't and, in any case, he just sat there open-mouthed, so I carried on.

"Bring together two pairs in the same reality and you get a big explosion that destroys both pairs. It's just reality's way of healing itself. But three of the same pair coming together – well, that's a bit more serious and reality will do it's best to make sure it never happens again, so it will make it so that the three items never existed in the first place. Why hasn't anything happened yet? Well, I knitted the last pair using a special slow-burn technique that I'd never heard of until I just invented it. Anyway, if you were only holding the three pairs of breeches, then you might just have got away with first degree burns, but I'm afraid that by wearing one of the pairs, reality is going to remove you from existence along with your breeches. I don't just mean that you will die, I mean that you will never have existed.

That is what I meant when I said that I was going to make sure that you never found out about the secret of Brindle Holm. If you never existed, then this can never have happened,"

It was at this point that the Nazi came back to life – a bit late, really, to be honest.

"I don't believe a word of it, you mad, old baggage. These are just knitted garments. Look, I've put one pair inside the other and I'm holding them both tight against the pair that I'm wearing. Nothing is going to hap ... who drew that handlebar moustache on the portrait of my beloved Führer?"

The last part was screamed from his now violently frothing mouth. I'd thought for a short while that he wasn't going to notice, which would have been a shame, because I wanted him to be *jolly* angry when he ceased to have existed.

Anyway, he stood over me and made to strike me with my own set of knitting needles – he was still clutching the pair that I'd accidentally left in the bag with the third pair of breeches, which I'd just nipped off to knit in the brief pause slightly before I'd pointed out the third knitting bag, just in case you're interested – at which point he stopped dead. Perhaps he'd just noticed that, although he'd stood up quickly and violently, the two pairs of breeches that had been on his lap had singularly failed to drop to the floor. Instead, they were stuck tight to the lap of the pair that he was wearing. It was at this point that he must also have felt some sort of stirring in his breeches and a look of blind panic appeared in his eyes. I don't suppose at this point that he'd noticed that I'd now added a sou'wester to my raincoat ensemble. Not that it mattered one whit.

Why the sou'wester, Dear Hearts? Well, it was all taking a bit longer than I'd expected and I'd just nipped off to the WC and back, in the brief second in which he'd stared down aghast at his breeches, and had added the sou'wester as an afterthought just in case anything in the vicinity of someone in the process of never having existed got messy. Anyway, he was still holding the needles, indeed, even though he tried to throw them away now, they seemed to be stuck to him as well.

Things were obviously starting to get a bit uncomfortable for him in the trouser department as well and I'm certainly glad that no-one came into the cell just at that moment, what with the Nazi screaming, "Don't think you'll escape me, you mad, old baggage," whilst trying to remove his breeches in an ecstasy of desperate fumbling. I mean, I'm a respectable cat, don't you know? Though I suppose that Lavinia is used to this sort of thing

Talking of Lavinia I've just remembered that time that we went ice-skating before the war. At the end of our session it turned out that someone had stolen her shoes from the locker, so the silly gel decided to walk home in ice-skates. All was well until we tried to cross over the tramlines at the southern end of Westminster Bridge at which point she got stuck. Well, I tried to get her out but her skates were well and truly stuck and she couldn't even get the things off because her feet had swelled up. Well, there was nothing for it but to give her a push toward the depot to see if they could get her out there.

Well, we'd picked up quite a crowd by the time that the inevitable tram appeared behind us. The driver decided to nudge up slowly behind Lavinia and gently push her the rest of the way, which was just as well because I was starting to get a bit worn out. The only bit of panic after this was when we got to the point at which two routes diverged. Well, one of Lavinia's legs stayed on the number 40 route to Lambeth, which was where we were heading, whilst the other started to head off south-west on the number 14 route. The poor gel nearly got split in two. Of course, the *Pathé News* arrived for a spot of filming before we'd sorted this bit out. Eventually, back at the depot, they got out some of those arc-welding thingies and we had a bit more excitement before we could get home at last. I spent the evening at the dear, old Trocadero, watching it all over again in-between Q. McLean on the jolly, old Wurlitzer and the main feature. It was *Room Service*, by the Marx Brothers, if I remember rightly. It wasn't quite as funny as the newsreel.

What's that, Dear Hearts, why am I telling you all about Lavinia when the story's just starting to get exciting? Well, it's another of those literary tricks that...oh, all right, if you insist. Honestly, I get no fun at all sometimes. Back to the story.

Well, to get back onto the point, Dear Hearts, I'm not sure that I ever want to witness the like again. All of a sudden, the breeches started to unravel – like a great, cosmic unpicking of an unloved and unwanted garment. Except that as the wool unravelled upward from the ankles the two garments stuck to the Nazi's lap rolled upwards and tied themselves first around the Nazi's torso and arms and, finally, head, before the whole ensemble unravelled completely into nothingness.

The Nazi seemed to melt, screaming into the wool as it unravelled. All that was left for a brief few seconds was his wool-enmeshed hand in mid-air, clutching the now glowing knitting needles. There was a last flash of light and the needles clattered to the floor. I picked them up and was startled to find that they pulsated with a life of their own. I suddenly noticed that where on each needle there used to be a neatly-moulded number "9", these had been replaced by neat, little swastikas.

I've tried to use them once or twice, but it doesn't matter what you start out intending to do, you always end up trying to knit a roll-necked, Kriegsmarine-style pullover and you get a migraine if you try to stick to your original pattern. Occasionally, I find them knitting all by themselves. Quite good, they are too, which perhaps says something for the Third Reich's monomania with once-popular folk practices, so as to in recreate an idealised Germany that never was. Well, even if many of old Mad-Alf's plans were barking, to say the least – I mean, making vegetarianism compulsory, I ask you – I have to admit that I'm all for keeping knitting in racial memory.

So what would happen now that I'd erased old Fritz, or whatever his name was, from history? Well, the cell disappeared and I was vaguely surprised to find myself back in *The Grimalkin* along with the Captain, thanking the landlord for such a pleasant stay. It has to be said that we all had slightly puzzled looks on our faces as though we all knew that something was missing and eventually the Captain asked what had happened to all those Germans, almost as though not quite sure that it had really happened.

"Oh, I sorted that out," I said airily, though with a bit of a puzzled look on my face as well.

"Yes," said the Landlord, "Though it all suddenly seems a bit of a blur."

Well, Dear Hearts, we headed back to dear, old Pill with a warm feeling in our hearts. After all, we'd prevented the Nazis from sinking our ships and also saved Brindle Holm from being occupied by enemy forces into the bargain. The Landlord of *The Grimalkin* – well, there I go again, Dear Hearts, I still don't know his name, and now the mystery is deeper than ever. I mean, if he was Landlord of *The Grimalkin* back in the late 18th century, how

Further Adventures of Tabitha Miggins...

on earth could he still be the Landlord in 1942? Or perhaps it was his day off or something. Sorry, I'm getting side-tracked again.

Perhaps the blur was something to do with the fact that as soon as the Germans had never come to the island all the beer had appeared back in the various public house cellars just as though nothing had happened – which indeed it hadn't now that old Fritz had been suitably excised from history. In fact, it was all seeming much more like a dream – reality was obviously healing itself and making some mental adjustments in people to make up for the current state of play.

For once, we decided to head back at night so as to get some proper sleep before the next shift on the Ferry. Of course, we'd have to sleep in our respective spare bedrooms so as not to meet ourselves before we went on holiday. Oh it does all get so complicated, Dear Hearts.

Well, we did our usual bit of piggery jokery in the Channel but something didn't feel right as we came back to the present day – there was a distinctly funny taste in our mouths. Well, everything looked alright, as far as we could tell in the darkness, but there seemed to be quite a lot of traffic up and down the Channel. We couldn't really see anything but just had the idea that there were more ships than usual at this time of night. It was almost as though lots of ships were patrolling, whilst not wanting to be seen. It was almost as if we were at war, I thought suddenly.

I felt a bit of a qualm at the back of my mind, but dismissed it. I mean, there was nothing in the history books about German Schnellboot attacks in the Bristol Channel, so it's not as if nipping it in the bud could have done anything too drastic with time. As we all knew, time is somewhat elastic and tends to sort things out to suit itself.

We reached the Avon and, as we headed upriver, the funny taste became stronger and stronger, as though some evil was emanating from somewhere close by. We moored up at Pill and the taste was almost physically overwhelming now. Whatever the evil was, it was as though its source was the Creek, which was ludicrous. I mean, there's hardly any Devil worship goes on up there nowadays, and most of the stray demons have settled down and got proper jobs now. Or did I dream that bit as well?

Well, we couldn't see anything amiss in the dark as we headed up to *The Duke* to see our friends and have an incautious chat about our recent goings on – we wouldn't meet ourselves because we knew that we were at a darts match at *The Railway* at this precise moment. This being Sunday, Belinda should be kicking off the dancing at some point soon, which will be very jolly after the unpleasantness of the last couple of days. Besides, we figured that a Milk Stout and an Old Silage would take away this awful taste, Dear Hearts.

    Well, we were in for a shock when we opened the pub door. *The Duke* was full of German soldiers. We stopped on the threshold and, just like in those old western movies, all the noise stopped as everyone turned to look at us. For a few seconds it was so quiet that you could hear a Ribbentrop.

6. Pill, Pill, ich liebe dich noch

Have you ever seen *Aliens*, Dear Hearts? No, I don't mean real, live aliens from another planet – and I'd leave off the calypso cigarettes for a while if you think that you have. I mean the follow-up to the film, *Alien* – and do you know that Jonesy was the only one from that film that was any good at acting in my opinion? I'm so sorry, Dear Hearts, I've got distracted again. What was I saying?

Oh yes, *Aliens*. Do you remember the bit where Ripley does that very slow and badly-acted double-take when she realises that she is in a room with thousands of eggs, and you have the feeling that at any moment they could all hatch and that would be the end of her? Well, that's exactly how we felt looking at all these German soldiers. I thought that I'd sorted all of this out and it was a bit of a shock, I can tell you, to find that I'd only sorted out the contents of the frying pan to somehow end up in a rather unexpected and much bigger conflagration.

We entered the lion's den and wandered self-consciously over to the bar. Still no-one spoke. Well, someone had to break the silence, otherwise I think I would have to scream. I coughed to clear my throat, but it was the Captain that spoke up.

"A Milk Stout and an Old Silage, please, Ralph."

We couldn't help noticing that it had got even quieter, if that were possible.

The landlord narrowed his eyes at us for a millisecond before he laughed out loud.

"You will have your little joke, won't you, Cap'n? You know as well as everyone that there are no such drinks." He looked at us with a slightly worried gleam in his eye and continued, "I'll get you both your usual."

The conversation started to build up again, but we could tell that there were still unfriendly eyes on us. One thing had broken through. There were no such drinks as Milk Stout or Old Silage. Now, that was serious. Well, whatever was going on, I'd got rid of Nazi infestation before and I was sure that I could do it again, but no Milk Stout. Well, I ask you, Dear Hearts, is such a state of affairs reasonable?

The landlord passed us over our usuals, whatever they were. Mine, the landlord pointed out, was an Erzatz Catnip Sling, as well I should know, evidently, whilst the Captain's was a frothing stein of some lager or other. The landlord smiled as he passed the drinks over to us, no doubt for the watching multitude, but his voice sounded anything but happy. I took a sip of my drink and was pleasantly surprised. You may remember my saying yonks ago – horrible word, don't know why I bothered to write it – that *The Duke* just couldn't get the hang of Catnip Slings? Well, this was much more like it. I'll have to see if I can't grow some of these ersatz things when everything's back to normal.

"Where the hell have you two been? And why come and make yourselves so conspicuous when you do finally turn up? And why did you call me Ralph?"

"Well," said the captain, tackling the questions in reverse order, "Because that's your name."

Reasonable answer, I thought, but the landlord's next remark was a bit of a poser.

"Don't be so daft, my name's Kyle, same as it ever was. What's got into you? You seem to be wanting to make trouble just for the sake of it. Come on, these beastly Nasties have got their suspicions of all of us in the resistance, so just keep a low profile."

"The path of least resistance, you mean?" I suggested with a twinkle - sorry, Dear Hearts, I sometimes just can't help myself, you know. The landlord just looked at me before he spoke quietly.

"Something funny's going on. You haven't been … 'got at', have you? I mean, where *have* you been for the last week?"

"Week?" said I. "We haven't actually gone yet, as far as we can tell – we're up at *The Railway*. At least, we thought we were, but perhaps we're not then. By the way, where are Belinda and Fernando? I would have expected to see them here at this time on a Sunday. And who are all these civilians that I don't know? Are they Germans too?"

"I don't know any Belinda or Fernando," said the landlord, looking worried, "And, apart from the Nasties, everyone else here has been a regular for as long as I can remember. It's you two that have only turned up in the last few years."

He goggled at us a bit as he said this.

We goggled back a bit, as well we might. Especially what with the Captain being Pill born and bred.

"Just out of interest, who *is* in the resistance here?" I said, as much to keep the conversation flowing as much as anything. The landlord – good lord, his name wasn't really Kyle now, was it? How awful for him – took a good look at us and decided that we were trustworthy after all.

"Everyone who ain't a Nastie!" he replied.

Which was just what I would have expected in Pill, to be honest. A new thought struck me.

"What about Mrs Posset's new baby?" I asked.

"Well, it's only two days old, so we won't be enrolling it for a week or so yet," said the landlord.

Anyway, several half-drunk Germans appeared at the bar for refills, still giving us what my Dear Mother would have called 'old-fashioned looks', so we decided that our first fact-finding mission of our new reality was over and took our drinks to our usual seats.

Hang on, our usual seats were in the snug. How did we know that these seats in the main bar were our usual seats? Ah, was time starting to heal itself? I hoped not, not in a reality where our friends didn't exist and where a whole lot of strangers, nice as they might be on casual inspection, seemed to be locals. To top it all, no Pill Brewery – well, no Pill Brewery beers on sale as far as I could see – and if that weren't enough, here we were being beset with these false memories as to our usual seats.

Sorry, Dear Hearts, technical term coming up.

'Oh gussets!' I thought, 'I really have messed something up, haven't I?'

Hang on, who on earth is Mrs Posset, when she's at home?

One thing I knew was that we were going to have to keep a hold of ourselves so as not to just slot into this particular unreality and forget about our own. I thought about things as I polished off my drink. One thing struck me immediately, which was how on earth could there be German soldiers here in Pill in the twenty-first century? What's more, they all looked exactly like they did back in the War – almost as though this was still the 1940s. *The Duke*, however, looked just as it did when we left – apart from the Swastika flag draped over the mirror behind the bar and the picture of Hitler over the door.

Hm, Hitler didn't look quite right now I came to look a bit more closely. He seemed a bit younger, if you ask me – as though someone had done a bit of creative portraiture, probably in fear of their life if they made him look too old. But how could Hitler still be alive? Oh, it was all too difficult! So I decided that I would slip back after chucking-out time and ask the landlord a few questions.

On came an Adge Cutler and the Wurzels song on the jukebox thingummy but, blow me, if after the well-known intro came Adge singing in German. No, I wasn't having this at all. Still, the Nazi contingent seemed to like it, banging their Steins together in time, more or less, to dear, old Reg's tuba accompaniment.

Meanwhile, I knew what had to be done, but there was a very large moral dilemma. To get reality back to rights would mean all of these nice people – all these locals I didn't recognise, I mean, Dear Hearts – no longer existing. I mean, if the Germans had won the War, which was how it all looked, then different people would have been killed and different ones would have lived, depending on the different circumstances. Probably many of those that lived through my war must have been killed in defence of their own country when the Germans invaded. In fact, I knew this for a fact – oh dear, here we go again, my mind getting used to these altered circumstances. What else did I know? Well, that the portrait was actually of Hitler's great, great grandson and not of Hitler himself. I wondered if he'd only been invited to one ball as well.

The captain chose just this moment to break in on my reverie and his thoughts chimed with mine.

"How long do you think we can stay here before we don't remember anything else?" he said.

"I don't know," came my reply, "But even if we were to head back to Brindle Holm tonight to plan how to sort this mess out, it wouldn't help. There are things I have to know first and things I have to undo."

The captain nodded.

"OK Tabitha, we'll stick around for tonight and head back tomorrow morning under cover of the fog."

Do you know, Dear Hearts, that that was the first time that he'd ever called me by my first name, and there I was thinking that he'd give me a piece of his mind for my having got the world into this mess in the first place. I asked what I thought to be a pertinent question.

"How do you know that there is going to be a fog tomorrow morning? I couldn't smell anything of the sort as we headed up-river. Well, I couldn't smell anything thanks to that awful, nauseating taste."

"Well," said the Captain, there's going to have to be a fog, otherwise we're not going to save the world, are we?"

Impeccable logic, I thought. Meanwhile, I outlined my plan.

"Tonight, I want to ignore all of these updating memories and get Pill's recent history first-hand from the landlord. Then I need to go and have very strong words with myself for giving me bad advice…"

I noticed the Captain goggling a bit at this.

"I'll tell you all about that later," I said, and followed this up with, "And then I'm going to have to do the fastest knitting that I've ever done. Really the fastest. So fast, in fact, that I unknit what I am knitting faster than I am knitting it. It's theoretically possible – not that I have the slightest clue what I'm talking about – but no-one's ever succeeded in knitting at faster than Warp speed before. But I'm going to have to manage it. I'm going to have to go beyond Warp speed and knit at Weft speed."

I thought that another Catnip Sling was in order, because I was having lots of very strange – well, I'm not sure what they were – I don't want to call them memories. Let's just say that I knew exactly what was going to happen tomorrow. To the minute – to the inch – to the stitch. I would be in time – no worries about sorting out all this changed history malarkey – it's just that after that I could see nothing whatsoever. Just a Miggins-shaped black hole; a singularity in the first person singular – and no-one to sing *Bushy Tails in the Sky* for me. Indeed, no-one, not even the good Captain, to remember me at all. It is possible to knit yourself out of history along with the garments that you've unmade.

So that was the price of one small mistake. Well, whatever happened to me, my course was set. That's what duty is all about, Dear Hearts. I made that a double Catnip Sling and knocked it back in one. Then I said goodbye to the Captain and went home to the complete Russ Conway collection that I knew I had in this reality – including the really hard one to find with Alma Cogan and Billy Cotton; not the Jasmine label reissue, either, but the real thing – and no time to enjoy it because of the music curfew in private homes that I also somehow knew about.

Further Adventures of Tabitha Miggins...

The moral aspect was getting to me a bit as I sat down in the familiar chair, though with unfamiliar furnishings. To do what I had to do consigned perhaps millions of people to death, or at least to unlife, or something. But others that died or were never born would get their chance. It did just cross my mind that in this reality *The War Between Cats and Dogs* might never have been made – I remember reading a local write-up that described it as a laugh-a-minute film and, after wasting all of fifteen minutes on it, had decided that the reviewer had only bothered to watch the first minute, after which inspiration seemed to have run out. On the other hand, I knew for certain that in this reality there was no *Old Possum's Book of Practical Cats*, which really did hurt. Now, I really do call that a rum tum tigger state of affairs.

"No," I murmured to myself as I made up my mind for the last and most definitely final time, "I lived through World War Two and I saw this lot of bully boys soundly beaten, so I don't see why, just because of one slight temporal faux pas on my part, they should have won instead. No, I'm going to do my damnedest to put things to rights."

I decided that it was time to go and have a chat with the landlord of *The Duke* before he went to bed and then to go and have that chat with myself. Just for peace of mind, I thought that I'd go and find out what happened to the Braun family in this reality as well.

Even though *The Duke* had been closed for the best part of an hour, I knew I'd find Ralph – well Kyle now, poor chap – awake. I put on my hat, left 1, Railway Cottages and headed down the hill. I decided to have a look up and down river before knocking on the door and this was almost my undoing. As I turned to cross the road to *The Duke*, two German soldiers moved in front of me and barred my way aggressively.

"Vere are you going?" asked one of the soldiers, obviously the brains of the outfit.

"I'm going to see Kyle," I said, raising my right paw to point at *The Duke*, which was directly in front of me and to the rear of the soldiers.

"See Kyle!" they chorused, stamping their heels together, one of them taking my hat off as they both raised their arms to point behind me, across the river.

"Yes, see Kyle," I reaffirmed, taking a step backward to pick up my hat and pointing behind them to show them that I knew better than did they where Kyle would be.

"See Kyle!" they chorused again, with the straight-armed pointing motif as before.

If the intention had been to knock my hat off again, I'd outwitted them this time by standing too far away. They still didn't seem to know where he really was though.

"Yes, see Kyle," I said, pointing in the right direction and feeling as though the needle had stuck.

"See Kyle!" they chorused again, pointing behind me in turn.

This went on for some time.

Eventually, I decided to change tack and said, "Well, I can't stand around chatting all day, well, night actually, nice though that is you Square-heads – oh, terribly sorry, force of habit from old Wagger Wagger Tagger, nothing personal – I've got to get going, don't you know? Well, toodle-pip and all that. As I've said once or twice already, I'm off to see Kyle."

As I pointed behind them once and for all, the two soldiers gave one last loud, "See Kyle!" still clicking heels and pointing in the wrong direction, though looking a bit tired after the last forty or so goes, then waved me on my way. Nice lads, I thought, but a bit dim. Funny, though, because I was sure that they would be just a mite suspicious of my late night comings and goings. I can't think what made them seem so happy with me.

I knocked on the side door – the secret knock for resistance business. I didn't even bother wondering how I knew this and waited for Kyle to appear. The door opened just wide enough to let me enter. Well, he'd been expecting me and we had an interesting chat where I found out quite a lot of curious things about this reality. Yes, it was undoubtedly my fault that history had been changed – there were certain large clues, which I'll tell you about in a second, Dear Hearts.

So why had I come out to see the landlord? Well, I wanted to find out about Brindle Holm in this reality. Did it exist? Did the Germans know about it? Was it still possible to reach it? That sort of thing. The answers were yes, no and yes, which was probably the best order for them. Kyle was in no way disconcerted when I told him that the Captain and myself were from a different reality. Said he'd guessed it must be that sort of thing for us to act so oddly. It takes a lot to fluster a Pill landlord – besides, I'd tried the secret sign of the Most Secret Society of Publicans on him and got the correct pawshake back, even though it is quite difficult, now that I'm getting on a bit, to get the other three legs into the correct position for that one. But, yes, it takes more than clashing realities to fluster a true Publican.

Asking further, it seems that the Captain and myself had left Pill a week ago to take some weapons to Brindle Holm out of harm's reach from Nazi searches and that we just hadn't returned. The same as in our version of reality, we should have reappeared about half a second after we'd left. The guess had been that we'd finally been rumbled and had been taken prisoner or had gone to a watery grave. I wondered if the other Captain and myself were having an interesting time back in our reality, or didn't it work like that? No, probably not, there were just one each of us, but different. The fact that I was about to go and see myself again was just another anomaly.

So, what were those clues that all this was my fault? Well, my history lesson was interesting. Evidently, Adolph Hitler had married someone called Gertrud something or other, who'd left her previous husband, one Wilhelm Braun, in 1923 for not being able to father children. Wilhelm had soon afterward been murdered by one or other of Hitler's stooges. Oh dear. So my clever trousers idea had all been for nothing. She, meanwhile, had then used her ruthless nature and her innate ability for thinking ten steps ahead (a rare ability, Dear Hearts) to change Hitler's entire strategy. Instead of invading Russia, he'd courted the US and they'd eventually come in on Germany's side. Britain, standing alone, hadn't had much of a chance. Then Japan and Russia had invaded the US.

The Germans had gone in ostensibly to defend the US, but had then joined forces with the attackers. Russia was nearly bankrupted by all this and it looked right here and now as though Germany was, instead of bothering to fight the Russians, just going to put in a bid for the country. What hope Japan after that? Oh yes, and China, without any foreign markets – not that anyone had any money left nowadays – was still a sleepy backwater. Communism had never washed over the country.

Well, all this warfare had lasted somewhere over seventy years at this point and thanks to the ongoing costs, innovation, enhanced though it had been by the war in the early years, was at the very tail end of the product lifecycle and had near enough stagnated. Hence the soldiers here in Pill

Further Adventures of Tabitha Miggins...

looking little different to those I'd seen in the Pathé film reels during my time in the ARP. Hitler had died a hero as had his son after him. His grandson was now looking close to being Emperor of the World.

Well, Dear Hearts, sod that for a game of soldiers! Even if I had to recreate a reality that included *East Enders*. At least I'd get *Emmerdale* and *Strictly Come Dancing* back.

I was just about to leave when there was another secret knock on the door. The landlord was expecting this and opened the door to let in a young lad of about ten. It quickly transpired that he was here to pick up a couple of rifles that had been dropped in for hiding earlier, right under the noses of the German imbibers. I asked him where he was going to hide them.

"In the loft, next to the tank," he said.

I was impressed at the thoroughness of the resistance movement here. I mean, where on earth could they have got a tank? Surely, the Germans must have missed it – and how could they have got it into their loft without being seen? Oh well, it was nothing to do with me because I was about to go and find out how to stop this particular reality from happening.

I took my leave of Kyle and left the public house by the back door, so as to avoid tiring out any more German soldiers with pointing in spurious directions, and headed uphill to the house that wasn't there. I made the secret knock on the invisible door and the shifting of the air told me that the door that wasn't there had opened to let me in. And not a slide rule in sight, Dear Hearts.

So where was I going? Well, I was going to have that little talk with myself to find out what on earth had gone wrong with my little plan. I headed out of the back door that wasn't there and ambled along to 1, Railway Cottages, which was that lovely shade of pink that I'd never have thought of using. I knocked yet another secret knock to tell myself not to answer the door, but to sit in the other room so that we wouldn't actually meet. Again. Then I opened the door with my key and headed indoors.

I could hear myself making a cup of doings and hoped again that there might be a cream cake in the offing again. I wasn't disappointed. A trolley appeared through the doorway, having been given a jolly good push by my other self. I stopped it and helped myself, pushed it back through, then sat down so that I could get on with some knitting as we talked. I could already hear the clicking of knitting needles coming from the other room; the sound stopped every now and then to be followed by a slight slurping noise and a click as the cup was replaced into the saucer. After we'd both done justice to tea, cakes and knitting, I poured another cup of tea and decided that it was time to kick off the proceedings.

"How is it that you didn't tell me that using three pairs of the same trousers would alter the course of history?" I asked.

There was pause before I – the other me, that is – oh it's so confusing, isn't it, Dear Hearts? – spoke with just the hint of surprise.

"Oh, did it? So you managed to get the plan to work, then? You see, I forgot that I would need to put a timer fuse on the second pair of breeches and blew old Fritz, or Günter, or Bing, or whatever his name was, to pieces long before I got to the third pair. Then what with the third pair being all alone in the world, they were harmless enough to pass on to Whitebeard next time I saw him to make up for his having lost the other two. Didn't I mention any of that? I suppose I assumed that you – well, me – would realise your – well, my – well, our mistake just a bit too late as well. Oh well, you live and learn."

We both drank to that. Then I headed back to the false present day for a couple of hours of shut-eye.

7. Tabitha Miggins changes the course of history (by design)

Well, we started out early next morning, just as though we were going to run the first Ferry of the day. A couple of things made themselves very obvious in the pale, early morning light. One was that there was a huge Swastika flag hanging over the viaduct. The second was that the Dalek on the other side of the river had gone. In its place was a very large Tiger tank, its nozzle pointing down river. Well, there's a nice Shirehampton welcome for you, I don't think.

We set across river with the first group of workers so that they could catch their train to Avonmouth Docks to do whatever it was that dockers did in this reality. As we started back, a thick fog appeared almost on cue. By the time we were in mid-river, we could see neither bank, so the Captain nosed us downstream. Quite how we got back to Brindle Holm I can't really remember because I was musing on such things as life and death. Both mine.

As I mused, Dear Hearts, it occurred to me that we have become accustomed to the idea that the proper way to die is peacefully in bed – as, indeed, I have on occasion. But the reality is that, for most of our various species' existence, death has been red in tooth and claw. The law of the jungle and so on. The only reason that we now think that a peaceful death at home is our due is that we haven't had one of those periodic frenzies called a World War for a while – at least, not in the real reality – and so we are startled every time we hear in the news of someone going under a bus or driving the wrong way down a motorway or meeting with a twelve-year-old meathead that has been brought up by similarly-meat-headed parents to think that the only way to survive the playground is to go 'fully tooled-up', as Willard refers to it.

In fact, the last so-called peaceful death here in Pill – the real Pill, that is – was far from peaceful, as I remember, and involved much recrimination from the soon-to-be-deceased about being more careful in future in verifying the freshness or otherwise of what had been a tempting-looking, but perhaps suspiciously-lone, piece of halibut in the fish mongers' window.

What it is to be wise after the event, but that's of little comfort when there is no future in which to apply one's newly-learned lesson, Dear Hearts.

Which brings me back to the here and now, which is that I know much better than to go and fiddle with the very fabric of history again, but in putting things right my time was now too short to ever be in need of that particular lesson again.

So, time to go and change the course of history again then, Dear Hearts. I'd better just clean myself properly behind the ears. Always go to meet your fate with clean Urals, Dear Hearts.

It was with a bit of a shock that I was brought back to my senses. I'd rambled off in my mind down memory lane for a while there before I realised that the Captain had been speaking to me for some time and that my ears were just about as clean as they could possibly be without taking the skin off.

"We're here, Tabitha," he said for about the fifth time. "What happens now?"

I thought for a second before responding.

"You head off to *The Grimalkin*. I need to do some piggery jokery to intercept myself with the third pair of knitted breeches before I undo removing old Herman, or whatever his name was, from reality. You might as well stay in this reality in comfort for a while – no Nazis here – ah, but no Pill Brewery beers either. Hopefully, I'll change that last bit."

I could tell that he wanted to ask the question of what would happen to us and wished that I knew. At least, I knew what would happen to me, but I hadn't bothered to tell the Captain because he'd probably try to stop me or otherwise do something equally sentimental and silly. But as for what would happen to the Captain, I didn't know. I hoped that he wouldn't wink out of existence with me and I rather vaguely thought that he'd just pop back into the right place once I'd put my mistake right. Probably.

"I don't know," I said to the unasked question, "But it's all been jolly interesting, don'tcha know? Wouldn't have missed any of it for anything. Got to go and put things right now."

Now it came to it, I was finding it rather difficult to say goodbye. Only one thing for it, and that was to turn away and wander off toward Brindle Hill and hope that I chose the right direction. It was all getting a bit difficult to see what with the lump in my throat and the tears in my eyes. It didn't matter what happened to me, but the thought of the Pill Ferry with no ship's cat rather upset me. How would the Captain get on? There was a sound like a foghorn as the Captain blew his nose so as to cover up the fact that he was a bit upset as well.

"Lavinia's a jolly decent sort," I said at last, "And she'd probably get the hang of things eventually. Though I'd get a couple of spare Ferries first, just to be on the safe side."

"Don't be silly," said the Captain. "It's a Miggins or no-one on the Ferry, as well you know. I'll see you in a few minutes. We'll meet again, somewhere or another."

And with that he waved me a confident farewell and headed toward the snug, bawling his eyes out, which rather spoiled the intended effect of nonchalant confidence.

Well, here goes.

I thought myself back to the 31st of February and headed up Brindle Hill, just behind the village, to the highest point on the island. There I was silhouetted just ahead, knitting the third pair of breeches furiously. In fact, I was knitting so furiously that I barely noticed when I merged with myself, apart from an almost imperceptible mental nod.

What's that? How did the merging happen? Haven't a clue, Dear Hearts.

Well, I'd been knitting furiously just now, but I knew that I had to knit like I'd never knitted before so as to both knit and unknit the breeches at the same time. We were both there at the same time, both in the same body but knitting in different directions. What didn't help was that time seemed to be doing some funny things. The other me seemed to slow down to the point where I could hardly see myself moving. It was a race to unknit the almost finished breeches. I had to start at the exact split second between finishing and casting off. Ah, here we go...NOW!

Well, Dear Hearts, the faster I unknitted the closer I seemed to the actual moment of cast-off. I sped up and the breeches unknitted themselves whilst at the same time still existing in completed state. Then things started to get a bit blurry as I approached and then passed Warp Speed and headed into the unknowns of Weft Speed. Thunderclaps burst all around me and visions came and went.

I was outside of both versions of me, watching the unknitting nosing ahead, unstitch by unstitch as the split second to cast off stretched out longer and longer. I knew I'd get there and then cease to be, unknitted out of history, but that didn't matter. Nothing was real. Nothing mattered. I seemed to grow vast and found myself bestriding the whole history of Brindle Holm, all at the same time, with lightning playing around my temples like a supercharged tiara.

I watched as the island was formed, thrusting upwards from the sea as tectonic plates did whatever it was that tectonic plates did – I always thought that they were something to do with poor service and having to wait an age before your meal arrived – and by the look of it, Brindle Holm started life as a last but rather more magical outcropping of the Mendip Hills.

I saw the first inhabitants arrive in what looked like coracles, those that had survived the crossing, that is. I wondered idly if they were allegorical coracles on the banks of the River Severn. Probably best not to analyse any of this, Dear Hearts. Much of what I saw I didn't understand: the stricken King with the bright sword, the sword being thrown into the sea, the hand in simmering Marmite catching it and disappearing from view beneath the waves, the King entering the cleft in Brindle Hill, right between my toes, and going to sleep. He'd catch his death in there, I thought; it all looked so cold and miserable and long ago. The carpenter arriving, lost in a boat from far away, and the Captain and I taking him across to ancient Glastonbury, where he gave me a very nice cup as a present. It was all he'd had left, apart from a very odd walking stick that caused no end of trouble every time he put it down on the ground. He'd bartered all of his other possessions for provisions before we'd headed toward the Somerset shore. Do you know, Dear Hearts, that that is my very favourite cup? It holds exactly a third of a pint and just feels right in my paw. Oh well, I don't suppose that I'll ever feel it in my paw again.

And still the visions went on. Other visions; other times; other ways – or autre temps, autre mœurs. I suddenly remembered Lavinia's take on this phrase – autre toms, autre paws. She doesn't know, but I've left my cottage to her, I wonder how long it will be before she manages to burn it down.

Anyway, back to being somewhat larger than I'm used to, I suppose that I must have been visible to all the inhabitants as I bestrode the island's history, which probably explains why the more primitive ones built shrines to their giant cat goddess. I mean, I might just have been a hallucination, brought on by too much ergot in the diet, or whatever, but you never know, do you Dear Hearts, and it's always best to be on the safe side. Those from less superstitious times probably just locked themselves indoors until the electric storm of a lifetime had passed. The knitting needles looked, as I watched myself, just like a single entity. Just as though I was holding a single dagger out in front of me, instead of, as it was, two needles, both going faster than sanity could grasp. Other parts of my life weaved in and out; I distinctly heard the Captain calling "Din-dins" to me through his megaphone at one point.

Another thought struck me. The cat and the island are one. So what will happen to Brindle Holm when I twinkle out of existence? Well, we'd see – or, more likely, I wouldn't see, thinking about it. Oh well, that can't be helped.

And there, in front of me, in the very fabric of time and space, opened a small tabby-shaped hole, complete with space for hat, whiskers and knitting bag.

'So this is the way my world ends,' I thought, 'Not with a bang, but a whisker.'

Either I started to get closer to the hole or it grew to accept my now rather large self as I came to the last few stitches – well, the first few stiches, thinking about it. Oh well, it had been a good life on the whole, I thought, as I got to the first stitch and prepared to cast on. Backwards.

The hole now seemed close enough to touch and was completely black on the other side. So black that you couldn't conceive of anything more black existing. What we call black night is as nothing compared to the blackness beyond the hole. So a nice, neat ending and no-one would have to grieve over my corporeal remains as tigger mortis set in. Or perhaps it would be another beginning. Perhaps the hole was just a time gate to other things. Who knows? Ah, here it comes; we'll find out one way or not in a couple of moments

Just at that moment yet another thought came to me.

"Oh you are a silly, old fool, Miggins! Always looking for a complicated answer to a simple problem."

It suddenly struck me that all I needed to do was to not give the Nazi the third pair of breeches and just let him blow himself to bits on two pairs, which would mean remembering, in the nick of time, to forget the timer fuse for the second pair. Then I could give this pair to Whitebeard quite safely. I'd already given myself the clue in my little chat with myself. Why hadn't I thought of it before now? Oh well, better late than never. Or was is already too late?

I paused as the first stich was about to unravel and then started to knit again in the correct direction. The tabby-shaped hole seemed to wink at me before it started to recede. As it did so, I got smaller and smaller and turned into a plain, ordinary cat again, with all relevant paws on the ground. Except for those that were involved in the knitting, that is, Dear Hearts. Both of me cast off at exactly the same moment. There, a perfect pair of knitted breeches with a lovely herringbone pattern. Again.

Such a nice, sunny day it was, and not at all stormy – no lightning around my brow nor the great, great, great grandfathers of storm clouds all around me. And best of all I could see my life heading on ahead again.

I thought myself back to 1942, the real one, that is, not the one in which I'd recently left the Captain, and looked down the hill at the cell where I was currently still Nazi-baiting. There was a sudden explosion and I realised that I'd gone and forgotten to add a timer fuse to the second pair of breeches this time around. Now there was lucky.

I decided to head into the cell to have a word with myself and to let me know that it would all be alright in the end, but as soon as I appeared I seemed to pop back into the one body – though at least it was the right one this time. Such an odd sensation, just like the first time I tried escargot, only I wasn't sick all over the table this time, Dear Hearts.

What with such a coming and going in various versions of my body I was starting to wonder which one was really me. I don't suppose it matters, really, does it? I only seem to remember one me at a time. Mostly, anyway. I have to admit that I was jolly glad for the plastic raincoat and sou'wester with this particular ending.

Now, something I'd forgotten about – I'm sure it's already occurred to you, Dear Hearts – was that now that I'd put reality back on the right track, we still had the rest of the Schnellboot crew to sort out. Somehow, I knew that the full complement of bodies should be twenty-one – how on earth did I know that, I wonder? – so there would still be twenty German sailors to account for before all was safe.

Well, it wasn't long before I was to meet some of them. The cell door was thrown open by several half-awake-looking chaps, who'd all run as fast as their legs could carry them from their various lodgings down at the harbour. One thing that pleased me no end was to notice that they all looked oddly relieved when they observed bits of fanatical Nazi all over the place.

"Schöne Tapete," said one of them, "Was für eine Schande über die Blut."

The rest nodded.

Well, the long and the short and the tall of it was that none of the other sailors really had quite the fanaticism of their Captain and just wanted to settle down in Brindle Holm. Being plain sailors caught up in a war they didn't particularly like, the place, what with its intrinsic links with the sea – difficult not to have them, what with being quite a small island, Dear Hearts – spoke to them. It also seemed that they'd all found themselves local girlfriends as well, which was quick work as they'd only been here a couple of days, but that's sailors the world over for you, not to mention girls living within half a mile of a harbour the world over too.

Well, there didn't at that point seem to be much more to say, except that the Pill Ferry Company bought the Schnellboot and hired it out for fishing trips as well as bringing it along to the Pill Regatta every year. But I'm getting ahead of myself here. Back in the here and now, I suddenly remembered the Captain and wondered whether he'd popped back into the right place alright. I got the key to his cell from one or other of the German sailors and we all headed next door. I was extremely relieved to find that he was there, still fast asleep after his somewhat strenuous arrest.

So, everything was back to normal again, I hoped, and I couldn't help but think that the fates had been kind to me.

"Well, well, well – c'est la vie," I said, almost to myself.

"Ja? Was wollen Sie?" asked one of the sailors.

"Oh, sorry, I wasn't talking to you," I said as our voices woke the Captain.

"Hello Tabitha," he said feeling the back of his head. "I've had a jolly funny dream all about another Pill. Well, it looks as though you've got all the Germans on your side. I take it that you've managed to sort things out whilst I've been having a bit of a nap? Did someone hit me? My head hurts fit to burst. I think a drink is called for."

"Yes, yes, yes, oh how sad and what a jolly good idea," I replied, which seemed to say it all. I hope I got it all in the right order.

Meanwhile, plenty of locals had now arrived on the scene. Were they back in charge again, they wanted to know, and could we let Whitebeard and his crew out of the lock-houses?

I waved the Captain and the Germans off to *The Grimalkin* and said that I'd meet them in a few minutes then went along with the crowd to release Whitebeard and crew because I wanted to see if things were going to go badly for the remaining Germans. I hoped not.

Whitebeard and his crew were out for blood as they were released, so I thought that I'd sweeten Whitebeard a bit.

I explained that the main protagonist had met his just deserts and that the rest of the sailors had just been following orders. I explained that I'd had to destroy his special breeches, both pairs, but that here was a little something to make up. Before we all headed to *The Grimalkin* I handed Whitebeard the new pair of breeches that I'd knitted, unknitted and knitted again.

"Why thank you, Tabitha," he said, "They're just like the ones that that nasty Nazi stole from my room. I could see him strutting about in them from my cell."

As his men were released from the various impromptu lock-ups that the Germans had contrapted I looked to see how Whitebeard's mother had fared. If you remember, Dear Hearts, she had once beaten me in a knitting contest. Well, when I say 'beaten' I'd won morally, of course. Her offering had been slapdash in the extreme, whilst mine own had been pure quality, but I digress. Well she seemed to be amongst the missing.

"I can't see your mother anywhere," I said.

Whitebeard looked at me for a few moments before he spoke.

"My mother is no longer with us."

"Oh, I'm so sorry," I said.

A rather inadequate nothing, I admit, but the best I could do, though further thought was rather prevented by Whitebeard's next response.

"I'm not," he said with feeling, "We left her at home because she's getting to be too much trouble on voyages. Getting drunk, fighting and knitting four-fingered mittens for the crew, that sort of thing."

"Well," I said, after a certain amount of thought, "We all have off days. And anyway, she could always unpick the mittens and start again when she was sober.

"Not my mother's style," said Whitebeard. "One of my men complained to her and do you know what she did? Cut off one of his fingers and told him that the mitten would fit fine now."

"And did it?" I asked despite myself.

"Fair to middling," was Whitebeard's reply. "Once we'd staunched the blood. Of course, then he cut a finger off his other hand to make the other one fit as well."

He thought for a while before continuing.

"My mother had knitted one chap a pair of mittens with no fingers at all. He was just about to go and cut all his fingers off when I thought that I'd better intervene, otherwise none of my crew would be fit to do any work the way things were going."

"What did you do?" I asked.

"I said they were ankle socks."

As we arrived at *The Grimalkin* it was evident that the remaining German sailors, standing outside and awaiting opening time, had worked out that they were not in the best of situations. They all looked a bit tense as the pirates muttered and glared darkly at them.

Whitebeard went forward ahead of his men and looked the Germans up and down.

"Right," he said, "I'm twenty men short for my next voyage – that's the reason that we put in here in the first place, to find a few sturdy, reliable men, and not like that last lot from that *Marie Celeste* ship – the useless buggers couldn't even moor their own ship properly without it drifting off in the night. You lot look a lot more useful, even if you've all got silly accents. I know already that you're good at taking orders, no matter how much mindless violence those orders require on your part. Excellent attributes I'd say. Who wants to be a pirate, then?"

Well, the Germans didn't need much prompting. Even those that didn't speak English well enough to follow what was being said figured that putting their hands in the air, just like their more clued-up compatriots, was a good career move at this point.

"Right, that's settled then," he said before turning to his men. "You can beat them up quietly at some point later in the normal course of your duties, but remember that they're your comrades now, so just a friendly drubbing is enough. Meanwhile, let's get down to some serious drinking."

Further Adventures of Tabitha Miggins...

Now that was what I called a good idea – and I knew a good way for the German sailors to start making amends for having pointed guns at us and for hitting the Captain on the head.

"Your round," I said, choosing one of the sailors at random.

"Nein, ich bin sehr dünn," he said looking a little confused.

Some people will say anything to get out of paying, so I peeled off a handful of Pill Pounds to pay for the first round and we all lived happily ever after until closing time now that we'd found all the Pill Brewery wares that had been diverted to the Germans' boat.

Oh yes, there was just one last thing that remained unanswered. Can you remember what it was, Dear Hearts? That's right. Why on earth were Whitebeard and his crew here in 1942 in the first place? Can you guess?

Well, there was quite a simple answer, which was that they've always got so much ill-gotten wealth that they have to spread it around so as not to cause a glut in any one time, which would bring the value down. Now that's what I call eminently sensible thinking.

Ah, there was just one other loose end to sort out as well. I'm afraid that I was going to have to give Wilhelm some bad news about his son.

* * *

I knew what time the meal was, so I made sure that I was at the door just as the bowls were put on the table. Now, I wasn't looking forward to giving the bad news, so I'd taken Sticky Paws along as well for moral encouragement, only he didn't seem to be around quite at this moment.

Still, I knocked hard and Wilhelm answered the door. I don't suppose he even saw me. It was the faked-up, official-looking telegram in my hand that was the focus of his gaze. He knew what it meant and he called Gertrud. They opened it together, trembling, as I tried to say soothing nothings. They read the telegram. It had taken ages for Sticky Paws to forge it and it was full of language to make any parent proud of their child's final moments.

Yes, he was a monster, as was the mother, but there are times to let the truth slide a bit. They said nothing other than to thank me for bringing the news so promptly, closed the door and took their grief inside. Ah, Sticky Paws was back from wherever it was that he'd just got to, so we could head home now with the episode fully finished with.

The following days were not very good for poor, old Wilhelm. Not only did he have his son's death to grieve him, but he then had to cope with Gertrud's suicide as well.

Suicide? Well, yes, quite why, otherwise, would she should have put poison in her borscht. I mean, it's not as though the poisoned portion could have been intended for her husband and that someone had swapped the bowls around, is it? No, the news must have sent her plain round the twist. Mustn't it, Dear Hearts?

That wasn't quite the end of the matter, though. I really had taken quite a liking to old Wilhelm and I asked one of the Captain's sons to go and have a word with him about a job. A job's just the ticket when you've turned inwards on yourself. Gets you back in the real world and lets you start to see things with a bit more perspective. As I'd expected, the job offer went down well and Wilhelm has just started on the *May King*, sailing between Pill and Brindle Holm.

Somehow, he's never on duty when delivering to early 1942. One day he'll have to find out the truth, but not yet awhile, Dear Hearts. No, not yet awhile.

8. Last orders for Tabitha Miggins

Well hello again Dear Hearts. Do you know, I'm afraid that it's that time again? Time for me to tell you about how I shuffled of this mortal thingummy again after meeting up once more with that dastardly Smuckle – though don't worry your dear, little heads about me, Dear Hearts, obviously I'm still here – or, at least, here again, or whatever – or otherwise who's telling you this story? Do think clearly, Dear Hearts! Such good training for later in life when all the muddle starts.

Besides, as you surely know, it's a well-known fact that cats have nine lives, though now I come to think of it, I can remember climbing up the curtain and joining the choir invisible at least fifteen times now. Basically, I'm just keeping schtum about it all and am hoping that The-One-Who-Runs-It-All doesn't replace his current, and rather ineffectual, database administrator, who's supposed to keep track of all this sort of stuff.

It has been said, rather unkindly of the administrator, even if fairly accurately, that he's so bad that he can't even access his own back end half the time. Oh, you didn't laugh, Dear Hearts. No, I don't think I blame you, on reflection; after all, as M. Clinton Jones said in his most wonderful book, *Database Design Made Easy*, there are no *funny* jokes about databases. That one included.

Anyway, as for the Supreme Being's database administrator, I'll tell you all about him later, because we meet up in this particular tale. In fact, you've already met him a couple of times, but I'll say no more so as to keep it as a bit of a surprise for when the time comes. Let's just say that he's more than capable of getting the query wrong and goodness knows how many lives I've still got left. Still, I'm not complaining. After all, there's still so much to do and so much good advice to give.

Anyway, this particular day started in such an ordinary way, as most of them do – unless you've gone and changed the course of history recently that is. I was up nice and early to bake my daily loaf and to enjoy a hearty breakfast of still warm bread with a hefty drizzle of Morningspill Farm honey. Yes, Dear Hearts, I know that the local GP told me that I had to cut out all sugary food – and alcohol too; well, the very thought – and stop eating a whole loaf every day because of the salt content or something or other.

Further Adventures of Tabitha Miggins…

Let me tell you that I certainly wasn't having that. I told him that I'd start listening to his advice when he stopped smoking 80 gaspers a day. Do you know, Dear Hearts, that he had the impertinence to say, "Don't do as I do, just do as I say," to that? Still, that's GPs all over. Cliché-ridden idiots, complete and utter ones; though stupidly well-paid and innately-arrogant, cliché-ridden idiots, it has to be said. It must be something to do with all the in-breeding within that particular class of society.

Anyway, one thing I *can* say is that I've never smoked a gasper in my life – well, except for that one shared with Lavinia outside the Festival of Britain, in 1952, of course, just to see what they were like, you understand, Dear Hearts. That was just before we headed in and had a go on the Waltzer. A bit of a mistake that, especially for everyone within a thirty-foot radius. Do you know, Dear Hearts, I've never been in the slightest bit tempted by the noble Nicotiana tabacum plant since then, having not the slightest wish to ever again see the same dinner twice?

Reminiscences aside, I'm – well, not counting various excursions into other realities and rather too many lives to remember – somewhere around ninety-five years old, Dear Hearts, and still in the rudest of health. I can't think why some nincompoop of a GP should think that I'm going to listen to the jolly bad and, unlike my loaves, half-baked advice of some young whippersnapper. I mean, why shouldn't an elderly person do pretty much what they want? Life's nothing but a series of giving up of things that you thought that you could never live without. Not that *I've* ever bothered with all that, Dear Hearts, but I do so hate listening to all of this from the inmates up at *The Home*, who always do what doctor says because doctor knows best.

Nonsense, is what I say to this; the only area in which I think that my own GP knows best is in which scheme to invest for best return – that and which private hospital to go to for specific treatment when *he's* ill. He certainly doesn't trust the NHS. As for doctoring, just remember, Dear Hearts, that 'GP' stands for 'General Practitioner' – they are not experts in anything but pushing their generally self-interested and unwanted noses into other people's lives for major financial return.

If you're not on a semi-lethal cocktail of tablets, then they'll get chased by various multinational pharmaceutical conglomerates to find out why. Tablets mean money. It might be life and death to us, the mere patient –

and often is thanks to being prescribed unnecessary and health-damaging medication – but it's golfing holidays (generally referred to as 'conferences', Dear Hearts) and final salary pension schemes to the average GP, all funded by whichever gigantic pharmaceutical conglomerate the particular GP has a 'special relationship' with.

Bung the silly, old biddy on all these tablets that are going to make her feel like hell. I mean, who cares? After all, she's only a silly, old bat. Never mind if that silly, old bat just happens to have won the George Medal for selfless bravery during the Blitz. After all, the GP wasn't alive then and doesn't have a clue about any sort of real life. A few hundred stiffs and a general poor quality of life for the rest on their account doesn't worry them in the least. They're all right, Jack.

Believe me, Dear Hearts, GPs are evil and are completely self-motivated – all but the dwindling number of caring, honest ones. You can tell those easily because they have nervous breakdowns within a year or two of qualifying, that or they turn into helpless alcoholics to try to blot it all out.

Those caring few aside, give me the Tabbyrigone's medicine man any day. All he is interested in is in making his patients well again, otherwise he gets his unmentionables cut off by the relatives of the deceased – and let me tell you, Dear Hearts, you don't practice for much longer after that. Minutes at most. A change of success criteria along these lines would do the average GP a great deal of good, as well as removing most of them from anywhere where they can do actual harm to the general populace.

I mean, I don't know why people keep demanding the right to choose euthanasia. All you've got to do is get a boil on your derrière, if you'll pardon my mentioning both objects, Dear Hearts, and go in to have it lanced. The sheer incompetence of a cash- and talent-starved NHS will see you dead within a week from there.

Oh, now I've got all angry about that silly medical profession again when I should be telling you all about my demise. Now, where was I? Oh yes, such a normal day and all that. Yes, back on track now, Dear Hearts. Just don't mention healthcare – nor children in public houses – and we should be alright from now on.

Well, we'd just started for the day when we got an All-Era call to help save the passengers and crew on an ill-fated, new-fangled passenger liner from centuries in the future.

Further Adventures of Tabitha Miggins...

What's that, Dear Hearts? What's an All-Era call? Well, it's funny that you should ask, because there had never been one before. But all of us in Pill – and Brindle Holm, as well as others in other places that have knowledge of and access to the...well, let's call them time gates for want of a better term – recognised it for what it was. An urgent cry for help at sea. Not that there was any sound. We all just knew. Who sent the call, or how, no-one knows, but when a sailor knows that others on the sea are in trouble, they'll drop everything and go.

And that's just what we all did, a whole flotilla of craft, big and small, heading as fast as possible down river to the Channel, through the Clevedon Flats time gate, to reappear in the mid- Atlantic next to a stricken and soon-to-sink liner. We didn't need telling that a storm was whipping up, meaning that we didn't have much time to help. Most of the boats, such as ours, were small and wouldn't weather the size of storm that we knew was coming. We just had to play our part and then head back.

From what was left above water, we could all see that the ship was gigantic. Much bigger than anything you could believe would ever put to sea. It was like a city, and like a city was a very odd shape overall. Not one of the rescuers was surprised to find that this giant beast was sinking because it didn't look as though it could have floated in the first place. Very un-ship-shaped and certainly not Bristol fashion. I found out later that the normal shape and rules didn't apply because it was powered and kept afloat by belief. It sank, from what I heard, thanks to an atheist in the works.

Some boats were already there, picking passengers out of the water, and others materialised at the time gate behind us as we headed into the action. There had been over a hundred thousand on the ship and sea was a crawling mass of people, all trying desperately to keep afloat. Hundreds went down before anyone could get to them. There was nothing we could do but pick up those we could and ferry them to some of the bigger ships that kept disappearing into the time gate when full only to reappear back through a split second later empty again. Someone, somewhere was wearing out his slide rule organising this one, Dear Hearts. Where or when the ships dropped off their loads of wet and exhausted humanity I still don't know.

The waves were already starting to get rough and we saw one of the rescuers from another boat being washed over the side. He wasn't far from us so we headed over and hauled him on board. We didn't pay much attention to him as we dragged him in, there was just too much to do, but I heard an intake of breath from him as he wiped the water from his eyes and looked at us. That should have told me something, because you could barely hear yourself shout above the gale that was now blowing. That must have been one loud intake of breath.

On that sound, something made me turn and look at him. What I saw, Dear Hearts, was a face that I'd much rather not have seen in the circs. Well, under any circs when it comes down to it.

"Smuckle!" I gasped. "So you're not dead after all."

I'd had a funny feeling about that, if you remember back to my first book, Dear Hearts – you really should read it, you know. Your life would be much richer for it, as would my bank balance, of course, and you wouldn't be so in the dark every time I hark back to it, would you? But, be that as it may, as to Smuckle, what on earth was he doing here? Well, just to remove any possible tension regarding the answer to that question – and just in case I forget to mention it later, of course, what with the rest of the story to tell and all that – we found out in due course that he just happened to be on the other boat in mid-Channel on the way from the mainland to his hideout on Lundy when it heard the call and he'd found himself here manning a rope whether he'd wanted to or not. But that's by the by for the moment.

The look on Smuckle's face said it all. Well, don't give 'em time to think of a nefarious plan is my motto. Well, it isn't, to be honest, but isn't that the sort of thing that you say in books? What's that, Dear Hearts? Please don't waffle on so when it's starting to get exciting? Well, I'm just doing another one of those literary tricks to increase the tension and all that. In fact, I *could* just finish here and leave you guessing until the next book? I could, you know, unless you leave me to tell things *my way*. Talking of which, I always did like The Peddlars' version of that particular song. So clever turning it into a slow blues, don't you know, well until the fast bit at any rate. What's that, Dear Hearts? Oh alright, back to the plot.

Well, the Captain was busy pulling another waterlogged parcel of humanity on board and wasn't aware of what was going on. It was then that Smuckle, pulling a gun out of what looked like a handily-waterproofed pouch, finally spoke.

"I told you that I'd come for you and the Captain, Miggins, and here I am. Say your prayers."

Well, all this was wasting time and I wasn't going to be thwarted in my attempts to save as many people as possible from a watery grave.

"Sorry, no time for that now," I said, "Here, hold this rope. Pull!"

"But..."

"No time for that either. Quick, pull!"

All of a sudden a wave washed over the Ferry and as I looked at Smuckle, I thought that I could see two of him, one whispering in the other's ear. I must just have had water in my eyes because when I wiped them with the back of my paw there was only the one of him of course.

Well, I was surprised at the change that seemed to come over Smuckle. The snarl disappeared from his face, the gun went down onto the deck, he took the proffered rope and started to haul away for all he was worth. The look on the Captain's face was priceless as he turned at one point to see who it was that was helping him to pull one particularly large and heavy chap out of the water. Still, being the Captain, he took it with a philosophical shrug and carried on with the job in hand.

We did three more runs to one of the big boats to offload our sodden and shivering cargo. On our way across to an area where we could see a group of people together in the water, *The Queen Bee's Revenge* passed by, Whitebeard's rufty-tufty pirates all buckling down to haul people out of the water. Well, what nice people they all were. Alright, so all the survivors' valuables ended up in various pirates' pockets, but you can't expect them to change overnight, can you? At least they were here.

On spotting the Ferry, Whitebeard waved to us and we pulled alongside to let him climb on board.

"My men know what to do, so I thought I'd come and help you for a bit – after all, there are only three of you. You could probably do with a bit of help" he said.

It was at that point that Whitebeard recognised Smuckle. I should add that they'd never met, but after hearing about our first acquaintance with him, Whitebeard had gone and taken a good, hard look at his face on the 'Most Wanted' posters outside the Bideford Militia's headquarters, just in case they should meet one day. Well, that day had come.

"What in the seven seas are you doing here? I'll scuttle you once and for all," he thundered.

Well, I reckoned that it was time for a spot of intervention again, after all we'd just arrived at the point at which we were aiming and there were people to rescue. One chap was already hanging on to the rope that I'd thrown out for him.

"No time for that, Teddy," I said, handing my end of the rope to both Smuckle and Whitebeard, "Pull together, you two."

"But..." he said, staring in exasperation at Smuckle, who was trying hard to look as though he wasn't there, what with having put his gun down earlier, to better get a grip of the rope, and Whitebeard currently having a serviceably-sharp, cutlass in his hand.

"No time for that either, Teddy," I said, "And do put that thing away or you'll hurt yourself if you're not careful."

This was almost too much for him, but after a brief expletive, away went the cutlass and the two of them buckled down good and proper. Quite a good team they made too. The storm, however, was whipping up and we had to leave it to the sturdier vessels that were designed for surviving all that the ocean could throw at it. So we put Whitebeard back on his own ship before we turned toward the time gate. That Smuckle was coming back with us was certain. I don't know why; I just knew that he was going to have a part to play in my future. My hope, after the sterling work he'd performed, was that it would be a good part.

We were almost at the time gate when a huge wave burst over the Ferry and Smuckle and I were both washed overboard. There was a riot of confusion for a few seconds as the water closed above my head. I somehow knew that we'd been washed overboard just as the Ferry went through the time gate. I hoped, against all sense, that the Captain would stay safe away from the storm on the other side and not come back to look for us. As I discovered later, he didn't have any choice in the matter because none of the time gates worked for a week after all the concentrated to-ing and fro-ing that day.

It must have been the weight of my rather sturdy knitting bag that pulled me down so quickly. I couldn't otherwise see any reason to go down that fast, unless it was fickle fate or some such thing. Well, there was Smuckle keeping up in the sinking stakes beside me; he didn't have a big, heavy

Further Adventures of Tabitha Miggins...

knitting bag, so I decided that it must be fate after all that was pressing its foot on the accelerator. Of all things, as we went down and down, faster and faster, it came as a surprise to realise that I could breathe – or perhaps it was that I didn't feel the need to breathe – and that I could see clearly, just as though the deeps were made of clear, early spring air. Now this was odd.

As I looked down I could see a public house on the sea bed. I couldn't read the sign without my glasses, but I thought that I could make a shrewd guess as to its name. It looked as though Smuckle was about to get his first drink in a long time. Here we were dropping down to come to a gentle standstill in front of *The Black Spot*.

I turned to look at Smuckle and saw that he was acting like an automaton, not like a real human being at all. He moved jerkily and glassy-eyed toward the front door and I followed on behind, wondering if I looked the same to him as he did to me.

Inside it was crowded and Smuckle automatically acknowledged greetings from various insalubrious people, some of whom I recognised as being his companions from his smuggling days. All, although acting as people do in public houses, were doing things in the same robotic way as Smuckle. Words were spoken, rude jokes were uttered loudly, but mechanically. No-one really seemed to be aware of where they were. Now I'm usually all for spending time in public houses, but I like them to have a bit more life than this.

'Ah,' I thought, 'Life is just what none of us have. That must be it.'

Of all things, as we headed in, someone took my knitting bag at the door. A doorman in a public house? Surely that was odd. A bouncer, perhaps, to either throw people in or out depending on the class of establishment, would have been rather more normal. Still, the normal rules probably didn't apply here.

As I handed the bag to the Eternal Doorman, as I suddenly knew his title to be, he laughed quietly under his breath, if breath there was, and my paw accidentally touched his hand. It was clammy and I was suddenly very afraid. Not afraid at this point of anything in particular, but just generally afraid. Perhaps if I could have seen his eyes I would have been reassured, but although I could see his whole face, I don't remember seeing eyes.

Smuckle was already at the bar, standing glassy-eyed, so I sauntered as nonchalantly as I could manage over to join him. Looking in the mirror behind the bar I was reassured to see that my reflection looked normal, or at least, Dear Hearts, as normal as it could under the circs.

A drink appeared in front of me, served by no-one that I could see, and Smuckle was already cradling his own drink in his hands prior to lifting it to his lips and partaking of his first drink on licensed premises since he had been burdened with *The Black Spot* by the Landlord of *The Grimalkin*. If you don't know what I'm talking about, Dear Hearts, then I suggest that you go out and buy my first book immediately. Let's see if we can get sales up to the twenty mark, shall we?

I picked up my glass and was surprised to see that it contained Pill Brewery Milk Stout. I was so surprised that I almost downed it in one, but something held me back. The general dread became very, very focused and I knew what it was that I was here to do. I was here to give Smuckle a second chance.

I put my drink hurriedly back on the bar and knocked the glass out of Smuckle's hand in the split second before any liquid touched his lips.

"Out!" I shouted at him. "Quickly!"

His eyes lost that glassy look and he spoke with what sounded like mingled regret and annoyance in his voice.

"I was looking forward to that." He said. "I haven't been in a pub for ages thanks, in no small way, to you and your frien..."

Then he noticed where he was. The look on his face would have been comic if only we weren't quite where we were. I seemed to know a lot of things suddenly.

"If we'd drunk just one drop here that would be to admit acceptance of death," I said. "And we mustn't leave anything of ourselves here, or we'll never make it back to the surface."

I made for the door pulling Smuckle behind me. He wanted to get out too, but there was something trying to keep him here. I grabbed my knitting bag from the Doorman's clammy hands and pulled Smuckle's black cloak from the rack behind the door. He put it on in something of a hurry, whilst I checked the contents of my bag to make sure that everything was there. I could hear gentle laughter again and then the Doorman spoke very, very quietly.

"You'll be back," was all he said.

I opened the door and pulled Smuckle out. As soon as we were through the door the nether world that we'd inhabited for a short while ceased and we were back where we should logically have been all along, which was deep underwater. Well, I couldn't see anything and certainly couldn't do much to help Smuckle from here. I'd got him out of *The Black Spot* and I hoped that that would be enough for the moment. I guessed which way was up and started to push for the surface. Smuckle rose with me, but I soon lost my grip on him. Minutes seemed to pass; I was desperate to breathe but knew that that would be the end of me because I was still far underwater. I must break the surface soon, I thought, otherwise I'm a goner, but unconsciousness came first.

I came to abruptly, aware that I was on a rock. So I'd broken the surface and been washed onto a rock whilst unconscious. Well, that was convenient. It was daytime and I could see that the rock was only a few yards across. Over on the other side, looking curiously at me was a puffin.

"Oh, hello," I said. "Do you know Belinda, by any chance?"

A funny thing to say, I know, but I still wasn't quite myself. I couldn't quite work out why I was here. I had some vague memories about a shipwreck and about Smuckle and about a public house on the bottom of the sea, but none of it really made much sense to me.

"Perhaps I've been having odd dreams," I said to the puffin, just for something to say, really. To be honest, I was talking to myself. "Well," I continued, "That's the last time I eat Limburger before bed, I can tell you."

The puffin looked at me in an odd way. I mentally rewound what I'd just said and could see that the puffin had good reason to look at me oddly. Then it was my turn to look at the puffin oddly because it had turned itself into a purple lizard of some description.

"How on earth did you do that, Dear Heart?" I began before the truth hit me.

This was a dream. I was still underwater and not saved at all. I knew what I had to do, but it was a wrench to do it. I let go of my knitting bag with my lungs almost bursting. It was no good, I had to breathe. I knew that it would be salt water that filled my lungs, but I'd got to the point where my body just had to do what it was built to do. I could not hold my breath any longer. I breathed the stale air out and breathed in.

And what I breathed in was air!

Further Adventures of Tabitha Miggins...

Admittedly there was a certain amount of salt water in the equation and I spluttered it out in a rather inelegant fashion, should anyone have been watching, which I shouldn't think anyone was out here in the middle of nowhere. But at least 90% of what had gone in was air. I'd broken the surface in the nick of time. I pinched myself, just to make sure that this wasn't another dream.

Ouch. I needn't have done that quite so hard, Dear Hearts.

The loss of my knitting bag was almost unbearable to think of, but, as I've always been taught, one that cannot cast adrift a treasure when there is need is in worse fetters than those physically incarcerated. Still, if I'd known how close to the surface I was I would have held onto my bag for dear...dear what? Dear life, I was going to say, but it would have been dear death. The extra buoyancy that letting go of the bag gave me was the difference between breathing in 10% salt water and breathing in 100% salt water.

I drifted for a while, though for how long I couldn't tell you, Dear Hearts, until I was eventually washed ashore on Brindle Holm. Long there I wandered, naked, it seemed to me, without my knitting bag. Brindle Holm was a bit odd, though, Dear Hearts, and seemed to be in some sort of in-between state. It wasn't like the Cat Heaven that I'd visited that time, if you remember the last book, and wasn't quite the everyday island as I knew it. Unfinished, it looked, as though the purpose had not quite been fully thought through.

This was explained fairly soon by The-One-That-Runs-It-All, when I bumped into him. He told me that the unfinished motif was because this was the bit that he lived in and that he couldn't make up his mind whether to do the place with flock wallpaper or anaglypta and, if the latter, was undecided about whether to use bold colours or pastel shades.

He also told me that I was, having been inside *The Black Spot*, technically dead, but that in reality I was here for a bit of a rest before being sent back to finish the job of saving Smuckle. He told me that the hardest battle was still to come. I'd already guessed that there would have to be one final battle and, from what he said, it seemed that it would happen in *The Duke*, back in dear, old Pill. Yes, that made sense in a way.

Anyway, whilst I was here I joined the Over-Heaven Redecoration Working Group and had some jolly good arguments with various other busy bodies that seemed to know nothing about decorating or design. It was just like being back in The Service, where everyone's opinion counted the same and where no one would ever think of actually asking someone that knew something about the subject. Such good fun, Dear Hearts.

Talking of which, why is it that all those silly students on business studies degrees never spot the fatal flaw in Belbin's rather weak-headed take on team formation?

What's that, Dear Hearts? What fatal flaw is that?

Well, it's just so obvious that I'm surprised that you even had to ask. But seeing that you have asked, Dear Hearts, what I mean is that nowhere does Belbin even consider the possibility that there will be at least one person in any team that is only there to amuse themselves at other people's expense. Honestly, hasn't Belbin had any experience of public administration or of higher education?

Why are students – and most of the so-called academics too, if truth be known – so uncritical about other people's ideas? Well, I suppose that being uncritical is far less work than using your brain, isn't it? What worries me is that students don't seem to go to university nowadays to learn anything. No, university is just a place to go and be entertained in-between school and the dole queue. Such a shame that the opportunity to grow the magic muscle, as dear, old Rustic Rod used to call the brain, is wasted.

Do you know, Dear Hearts, that I once wrote a very heartfelt letter to *The Guardian* about the current state of higher education? Not that they published the thing, of course, but it did at least help me to let off steam and get my blood pressure back to something akin to normal. The main gist of the missive was that, what with the prevalence of all this technology malarkey, the term 'reading for a degree', as still used rather endearingly on *University Challenge*, should be changed to 'cutting and pasting for a degree'. No wonder that the majority of young people leave university nowadays without even having found the library, even those that have the slightest clue what a library is.

Anyway, where was I? Oh yes, resting in the administrative and systems section of Brindle Holm.

Well, I nodded to The-One-That-Runs-It-All whenever our paths crossed and I was surprised when I got to know that he had a new database administrator. It wasn't so much the fact that there was someone new in post that surprised me, but that here I was technically well over my allotted number of lives without the error having been spotted by the new chap. Well, the big surprise was still to come when I found out who the new person was. It was Lavinia's Kevin.

He wasn't dead, The One told me, for which news I was glad, but he had been looking for work just at the right time. It seems that Kevin had been one of the many victims of a recent purge of all unnecessary Civil Servants following the appointment of a rather radical, new broom that actually knew what it was doing and why. Kevin had been deemed part of the useless 98%, most of whom were still on the job market. The only bit of news that hurt was finding out that the exceptionally important role of Colonial Companion had also been deemed superfluous to requirements. Well, the new broom may have got it right in Kevin's case, but The Service without Colonial Companions? I ask you.

Meanwhile, Kevin had got this job by one of those usual muddled chains of events that had always left both himself and his mother drifting on the seas of fate, rather like incongruous croutons in custard. All too tedious to go into now, but he didn't have the slightest clue about database administration and only applied because he hadn't read the job spec. properly and thought that the database administrator's role was to clean the thing rather than run it; you know, Dear Hearts, do the dusting and sweeping up sort of thing. So he'd applied in that occasionally endearingly-clueless sort of way. He shouldn't have stood a chance, but the thing is, you see, Dear Hearts, that The-One-That-Runs-It-All is one of those Old School sorts that doesn't trust anyone who claims expertise.

So Kevin had landed the job and the fun had started. He really didn't have a clue about what he was doing and all sorts of things went rather awry, such as Cat Heaven being concatenated with Mouse Heaven for a few interesting hours. Well, that was after spending the first few days with bucket and mop in paw, trying to find the database so the he could clean it.

Eventually, The-One-That-Runs-It-All had to intervene. He liked Kevin's sheer incompetence, however, and decided to keep him on, nominally in charge, but where he couldn't do too much harm, but to then clone him – after all, it really was too big a job for just one mortal – and genetically-moggify the clones so as to make perfectly-formed database administrators, complete with all the relevant attributes.

Further Adventures of Tabitha Miggins...

In all, four hundred clones were made, this so as to keep up with all the work of running the mindlessly complex relational database that keeps the myriad heavens working properly. The person that designed and built it in the first place had disappeared halfway through the processing of a fiendishly-complex analytical query – sucked in as a multidimensional parameter is the best guess. His record is still there but no-one can work out what the data contained in it means. And let that be a lesson to all database administrators. Just let the database hold the data, is my advice, Dear Hearts, and then filter the data and get it out into applications better suited to do the analysis. You'd have thought it was so obvious a conclusion, but no. Database administrators like to complicate every simple gift of the gods, probably just to keep themselves in work. Silly sods.

Except for Kevin, of course, who still doesn't have a clue what he's doing. Still, he'll probably do less damage that way ultimately. Anyway, he's only supposed to be in charge of the timetabling part of the database now, the bit that keeps track of which of his clones is doing which shift on which part of the database. In theory, anyway, because he'd just managed to give all four hundred clones the same fortnight off just before I arrived. It seems that they all have the same name – Kevin. And Kevin just thought that it was a system error and that he was authorising the same holiday request four hundred times. A plausible error, of course – databases are like that.

Well, whilst the clones were away I gave him a spot of help, sorting out some of his more muddled queries, which should have seen various heavens being a bit less full of different bits of each other's food chains. Wool, euphoniums and Pill Brewery Milk Stout mysteriously found themselves in the order inventory lookup for Cat Heaven after Kevin went off for his dinner break, leaving me to keep his chair warm. There's also a new table dealing with charabanc outings to other heavens as well, well to Pirate's Heaven, Ferry Captain's Heaven and to Publican's Heaven to be specific. I made sure that there were no audit tables before I updated anything; now that really was slack of the designer, I must say.

I didn't have to do anything with my own record because Kevin had already accidentally updated my *MaximumNumberOfLives* value from *=15* to *>15* at just about the time, according to the date stamp, that I was being washed off the Ferry. Now that's what I call good timing.

Further Adventures of Tabitha Miggins...

Well, that should keep me going for a bit – and I also built in a macro to daily refresh that particular part of my record with the current entry just in case anyone should spot it later on. The joy of macros, of course, is that even if you suspect that one is there, they're so hard to find. And no-one likes to delete them because of all the cascade errors that can cause.

Still, eventually came the day that I knew that I would have to leave and, to be honest, I was glad. Although I'd kept myself busy with a certain amount of creative database administration and straight-faced sabotage of working group meetings, I was missing my knitting bag. I'd not felt quite right since I'd let it go. That I'd lost it for good was gnawing at me and I didn't know what to do about it. I had a second-best knitting bag back in Pill. It wouldn't ever be the same, that much I knew, but I'd got to the point where I felt as though I was going to burst if I didn't get my hands around some sturdy handles pretty soon.

So we come, at last, to my latest resurrection, Dear Hearts. One moment I was wandering along the path toward the next Over-Heaven Redecoration Working Group meeting, thinking up a few subtle arguments to stall any possible decisions about what colour to paint the machine room where the mainframe was held, the next I was breaking the surface of the water, Smuckle appearing a few feet away from me a split second later.

Smuckle was unconscious and I was suddenly afraid that he might just go down again, so I kicked my way over to him, grabbed hold and looked around to see if there was any sight of land. About ten feet away was the Pill Ferry slipway. Well, there's convenient, I thought, Dear Hearts. It still took the best part of five minutes to drag the inert form of Smuckle over and far enough up the cobbled slope that the tide wouldn't pull him back in again. Luckily, the tide was almost at its highest, so I didn't need to pull him up too far.

A cursory glance told me that Smuckle looked rather more than half-drowned, so I thought that I'd better get some help pronto...except that there didn't seem to be anybody about. No-one, not a single, solitary person. Don't tell me that I'd somehow been and gone and changed the course of history again. No, it didn't feel the same at all, Dear Hearts. No foul taste in the air, nothing except the jolly invigorating smell of clean, fresh, Pill air. Ah, was that the sound of the harmonium playing up in the chapel.

Further Adventures of Tabitha Miggins...

I headed up the hill and entered the packed building. Everyone I knew from Pill was here, as well as a fair smattering of people from the surrounding villages. I realised that I'd just walked into a memorial service for all of those lost in the disaster – that seemed to be weeks ago to me – but time was obviously doing some odd things again.

I'd arrived just in time to hear the roll call of the dead and missing, the latter all presumed to be drowned. In all twenty of the would-be rescuers never came back. They started with those from other ports and villages. For Bideford they got to 'S' and out came Smuckle's name. Well, won't they be surprised when I tell them he's still with us, I thought.

Other local places that lost souls were Burnham, Lundy and Minehead. After Minehead, there was a pause before the padre spoke again.

"And from Pill," he started.

Oh dear, I thought, not some of our own. It wasn't the Captain, for which I was thankful, because I could see him at the front. Who could it be, I wondered?

"And from Pill..." he continued, "...Tabitha Miggins."

That brought me up with a bit of a start, even though I should, by now, have been expecting it.

'That's me,' I thought.

But I was only technically dead, not really dead. I mean, here I was and all that. And then I spotted my knitting bag at the front of the chapel in the place of honour.

So I *had* gone. Not just technically, but really. I was starting to wonder seeing as no-one seemed able to see me. I couldn't help but remember, as I looked at my knitting bag, sitting forlorn and damp at the front of the chapel, that it was my birthday, just to add that touch of symbolism to the occasion. Though symbolising what, I'm badgered if I know.

'So here I am,' I thought to myself, Dear Hearts, 'Not in the body, it seems, but rising, perhaps, on the stepping-stones of my dead selves to higher things, so to speak.'

I can't think why I thought something so foolish, but there you are, I was all of a doo-dah. It suddenly stuck me that although I was still here, there were some very significant problems around no-one seeming to be aware of it. Now I don't call this state of affairs 'higher things' – I mean, what's the point of being here if no-one can hear me ordering a Milk Stout now, Dear Hearts?

I carried on with a spot more thinking. I'd come here to get help for Smuckle, but it seemed that I couldn't get help as things went. So I sat and thought a few things through. Well, I knew that the Cat and Brindle Holm were one. Or, at least, I think that I knew that, though one knows how elderly souls, such as my good self, get these sorts of fancies from time to time. That matter aside, I suddenly knew one thing for certain, and that was that whether the Cat and the Island were one or not, the Cat and the Knitting Bag were most definitely one.

Of course, how stupid of me; that was it. I'd never felt righter. I'd felt rudderless since letting the thing go, even though letting go had been my only hope. I *was* dead without it.

The knitting bag was an heirloom from dear, old Auntie McAsser, and was presented to me the very day I was born. I used to sleep in it until I grew up a bit. Certainly, we'd never been separated before. No-one in Pill could possibly believe my being separated from it for any reason but one so the only conclusion that they could come to when finding it washed up in the Creek without me (how did I know that this was so, Dear Hearts?) was that I had shuffled off the perch. It was their belief in my demise that was keeping me in this state.

So here I was in limbo again. Dead for the moment, but with potential still. So how to get out of limbo and get help for Smuckle. I'd got out of limbo before, often, but never the same way twice; that's one of The Rules. Well, there was only one course of action as far as I was concerned.

I strode to the front and grabbed hold of the bag. The moment my paw touched the handle there was a curious popping feeling in my ears, followed by a gasp from the mourners. The padre kept on going a bit, not realising that events had rather overtaken him, until even he noticed that something was going on behind him.

I finally found my voice.

"Very nice memorial service, padre," I said, "I'm touched, but I'm afraid there's no time for that – there's a near-drowned man down on the slipway that needs urgent help; another one to take off your list if we're quick. Come on!"

Well, everyone caught the mood and no-one bothered to ask any questions, which was all to the good, because I wasn't really sure how to answer most of them at this precise moment - feeling dizzy and light-headed, I was, just as though I'd been and gone and had two rides in a row on the Waltzer, though, thankfully, not as badly as if I'd also partaken of one of Lavinia's Woodbines beforehand.

Anyway, everybody trooped out of the chapel and rushed down the hill after me to the Ferry slipway. My knitting bag seemed to pulsate in my hand with a life of its own, giving me the strength to outrun the crowd. There, just where I'd left him was the inert form of Smuckle. I hoped I wasn't too late. No, I couldn't be because the final battle had to happen in *The Duke*, just away across the road there.

Those with first aid skills did what they had to do and jolly uncomfortable it looked for poor, old Smuckle too. Kneeling on his stomach and pounding his chest to get the water out of his lungs and all that. Well, that's what it looked like from the back of the crowd, where I now stood quietly with the Captain.

"I thought we'd lost you that time," he said. "Though I'm jolly glad to be wrong. Let's head to *The Duke* and I'll buy you a drink to celebrate."

A man of few words, the Captain, but all of them good ones, you'll have noticed.

"I'll be very glad of one. Well, several to be honest. It's been a very long and tiring departure and restoration. But there's going to be a bit of difficulty to get over before I can have that drink."

It was at this moment that Whitebeard, who was also hanging around at the edge of the crowd with the Captain and I, finally got a glimpse of who it was being saved.

"It's Smuckle!" he exploded. "What on earth are you doing trying to save that scum? Here let me push him back in and finish him off this time for good and all."

He made to move but looked at me first, just to check if I was going to let him.

I wasn't.

"Oh, alright Tabitha," he said, spotting the look on my face, "Have it your way. So what are we going to do with him?"

"We're going to take him to *The Duke*," I said. "When he comes around, he'll need a drink."

Neither the Captain nor Whitebeard said anything, but I could hear them both thinking very loudly. I was about to break the most binding law of the Guild of Master Victuallers. Only sheer force of will, and a little centrifuge on my part would get me through.

Well, the willing hands that helped to carry the now slightly more alive-looking Smuckle into the snug of *The Duke* had no idea that what they were doing was wrong, indeed didn't have a clue who Smuckle was, so they can be forgiven. The Captain and Whitebeard remained quiet throughout. Condoning my actions through inaction, or just trying to work out what on earth to do about it? Doesn't matter really. As far as I could see it, Dear Hearts, getting Smuckle into the public house was the hard bit. Once inside such a place, drinking tends to follow as a matter of course. At least, that's my experience.

Whilst Smuckle was being made comfortable, both the Captain and Whitebeard headed straight to the bar, where they both bought and downed a large whisky each in double-quick time before buying another, which they both seemed inclined to nurse, rather than bunging them down the hatch to chase the others. Curious, I'd never known the Captain to drink spirits, except on special occasions; that or when he needed bracing.

It was at this moment that the group of people around Smuckle parted enough for the landlord to see him. 'Ah, here we go,' I thought. I asked for an unfeasibly large whisky along with a Milk Stout chaser.

"I can't do that, Miss Miggins," said Ralph, going all formal – I mean, first name terms with me usually. "You're intending to give a drink to that man and I can't allow that. He's been given *The Black Spot*. I'm sorry, but it's The Rules."

So my little try at centrifuge hadn't worked. Time, then, for plan B.

"Teddy," I said, "Your whisky, please."

Whitebeard started as though he'd been stung by a hornet – not one of our puny, little ones either, Dear Hearts, but one of those huge things that come and stare at you, from just close enough that your eyes cross, in certain less well-regulated parts of the world where hornets being six inches long seems to be standard. I'd rather put him on the spot, I must admit, but I thought that, what with him only being an occasional local, he'd be punished less than would be the Captain, who, along with my good self, was in *The Duke* at least twice a day.

Still, it was the Captain that moved first, irrespective of the consequences. The customer is not always right, and we both knew that we were certainly wrong here. But I'd decided that it was time to make a stand for what I knew was right. Bad boys can come clean, you know.

"Here," said that good fellow, "Take my drink, Tabitha."

I took it and started to walk across to Smuckle, at which point the landlord shouted.

"Time, gentlemen, please!"

Well, we'd heard the phrase many times before, but there was an odd inflexion that sounded more like a threat this time. I couldn't help but notice idly that his voice had been so loud that it had stopped the second hand from moving on the clock.

Then I noticed that it wasn't just the clock that had stopped. Everyone except myself, the landlord and Smuckle, who chose just this moment to groan, was poised in mid-whatever it was that they were doing when time stopped. The landlord spoke rather more quietly.

"I'm very sorry, Tabitha, but you really mustn't. I've had to call in a higher authority, because this is too difficult a decision for me. That man mustn't have a drink served by myself, whether on or off my premises. It isn't just more than my job's worth. It's more than my life's worth. If I allow him to be served, then my career is forfeit. And you know well that landlords work until either Death or Customs and Excise comes to visit. If I'm thrown out of the Order, then I might as well be dead. And I'm not ready to ring the bell for the last time quite yet."

Hm, I saw his point. I hadn't realised that it was quite that dire. Hang on, what was that about a higher authority? That sounded a bit worrying. Or did it? When it came to bunging difficult decisions upstairs, I reckoned that I knew a bit. My life in The Service had given me a great deal of first-hand experience of negotiation and reconciliation with higher authorities. Admittedly, that was usually, just before we sent the gunboats in. But did I have a spare gunboat about my person? Of that I wasn't sure.

I suddenly noticed that Ralph was looking past me at something. I turned slowly and was not really that surprised, when it came down to it, to see The Landlord of *The Grimalkin* standing behind me.

So, is he versed in the Black Arts of the Guild of Master Victuallers? Well, even if I didn't already know that he was, the badge on his rather fine and unexpected ceremonial blazer would have told me that this was indeed so. Well, as far as I knew – indeed he'd told me – he never left Brindle Holm if he didn't have to, so I guessed that something important was about to happen.

"Hello Tabitha," he said, "Well, you're trouble today and no mistake."

This was going to be difficult. Fond as I was of Ralph, well, I was perfectly prepared to steamroller him up to a point. But The Landlord was a bit different. A real friend, he'd become, over the last three hundred years or so. I prepared myself for a difficult conversation.

"Oh, how nice to see you here," I said, testing the water a bit before coming to the meat of the matter. "I'm just going to give Smuckle this drink that Ralph kindly poured for the Captain."

I wanted it made clear that Ralph was in the clear as far as I was concerned. One always has to play the game fairly, Dear Hearts. As I took a step Smuckle-wards I decided to try a little syllogistic horror on the Landlord. Well, you never knew.

"If," I started, conversationally, "If *The Black Spot* can only be given under specific circumstances, as you once told me is the case, Dear Heart, then, logically, it should be possible for it to be revoked in special circumstances as well. Just because it's never been done doesn't mean it can't be done."

I tried to keep a quiver out of my voice and even managed a couple more steps toward Smuckle before The Landlord said something that stopped me dead in my tracks.

"Okay," he said, "That's fine with me."

I was so surprised that I dropped the drink.

"What?" I said in stunned tone, as Ralph poured another very large whisky, "It's as easy as that? Doesn't it need to go to 'Senate' or 'Council' or whatever it is that The Guild of Master Victuallers has?"

"No need. I'm the Grandmaster of the Guild, have been for centuries and will be for centuries more. What I say goes and what a Miggins asks for tends to get done."

So The Landlord was the one that makes The Rules, the one that battles, at the strategic level, obviously, with the Dark Forces of Teetotalism and

Nitrokeg. As I found out a little later, he was also the author of *Inn Keeping and Wild Romaunce*, a curious little tome that seems to randomly mention parrots and herb lore rather a lot amongst various tales of derring-do by members of the licensed trade during the normal course of their duties. More power to his elbow is what I say.

What's more, he made me an honorary member of The Guild and gave me plenipotentiary powers to alter the rules as and when I felt it necessary. He said that every landlord in the Seven Kingdoms would recognise my authority, even as they could recognise someone that had been given *The Black Spot*.

I was just about to ask which Seven Kingdoms these were exactly, but it suddenly struck me that there was a sick man to be given a drink. Time restarted. The Landlord wasn't here, Ralph hadn't shouted and I happened, curiously, to be in exactly the same place as I had been when he had.

I gave Smuckle the drink. Well, poured it into his mouth to be honest – not really much else I could do. All was well for a few seconds at which point his eyes opened and he stared wildly. Then he threw up a mixture of whisky and sea water. And after all I'd done to get that whisky down him as well, the ungrateful sod. But it got him coughing and soon he was sitting up. Whitebeard got the next drink to stay down. Ralph, meanwhile, made things official.

"*The Black Spot* has been revoked. Hebediah Smuckle is perfectly welcome in every pub in the Seven Kingdoms."

Well, there it was again. Whilst Smuckle was catching up with reversing several years of sobriety, I asked Ralph what the Seven Kingdoms were.

"Haven't got a clue," said that worthy, "It's just what I have to say for any bit of Guild law. If you want to know, you'll have to ask Old Nick."

"Who?"

"The Grandmaster."

"Oh. So that's who he is."

Well, if that's the case, which wouldn't really surprise me – I mean, I know the other one as well – I think that I can guess at least one of those Kingdoms, Dear Hearts. There's only one public house there, and that only on the way in.

Further Adventures of Tabitha Miggins...

9. Epilogue

So what of Smuckle, I hear you ask, Dear Hearts?

Well, Smuckle started a mail order company using our anomalies in time to sell perfect condition original vinyl records and Hornby-Dublo, Tri-ang and other railway models in the present day. Not really within the spirit of the thing, I'd have thought, but there you go.

He uses the Internet to buy collections of old money, going forward in time to when the collector's market for old notes has completely died and there's no demand, so getting the £sd for a song, then goes back in time and buys the items at trade price. He's making an absolute killing. It's an interesting business model, too. He doesn't tie himself and his money up in lots of stock; instead, he advertises mint condition items without actually having them and when the money arrives he pops back in time and buys whatever it is direct from the manufacturer. His feedback is exemplary as well because he knows exactly when payment arrives, so then organises things so that the items arrive by courier the very same day as payment is sent. He got himself a team of side rule manipulators to make all of this possible. And you should just see the model railway in his loft as well, though what he sees in the Battle Space range, I really don't know. On the other hand, I do like the wagon with the giraffe that ducks its head to go under the bridge.

But I digress, when it comes down to it, Smuckle has that sort of mind that skims straight to the essence of any opportunity. He fitted seamlessly into the 21st century world, with hardly any culture shock at all, and just seemed to know what all this technology malarkey could do for him. Devious too; do you know that he even goes back and commissions short runs of locos that were never made, but which devotees wished had been.

He fairly quickly, once discovering about the change over from £sd to decimal coinage, had the idea of going to the Treasury in advance of decimalisation and asking to buy all the old currency for 'sentimental reasons'. The Treasury thought that they had a nutter to deal with, what with wanting to give good, new money for worthless old. He got it all for a song, pretty much, what with saving the Treasury the cost of destroying it all. Well, Smuckle kept a small amount back for trading in the past – a couple of million or so – and immediately went back to 1966 to open a savings account with the rest – good interest rates in those days, Dear Hearts – and when decimalisation arrived in 1971 it all got converted into new money, of course. In fact, it was some of his 1970 interest that he used to buy the old currency with. I wonder if the Treasury ever worked out that the amount they sold to Smuckle was almost exactly how much more money there was in circulation at decimalisation than they'd expected. No, I shouldn't think so for a moment either, Dear Hearts.

Not long after he employed a team of techie whizz-kids to design and develop a time gate app for mobile devices so as to make all that coming and going in time less complex. You just type in where and when, along with any other parameters, such as not wanting to meet yourself, and it sends you there to the microsecond. Even the Captain has forsaken his slide rule and he's as pleased as punch with his new tablet because Smuckle has also added the complete works of Hal Jons to the thing, so that the Captain can read his favourite books wherever he is. The only problem is remembering to plug your device in regularly because you can end up in some funny places when you're on low charge.

Oh, before I forget, I think that I mentioned in my first literary outing, Dear Hearts, that it is sometimes difficult to know, what with all the gadding about in time and space, quite when you are meeting people. Even if you know them very well in your own chronological time, are you meeting them now for the first time from their point of view? Well, I suppose that I should have been a bit more cautious when I spotted Smuckle a few weeks ago, especially as we were both a little off the beaten track as regards the Pill of today. Indeed, it was whilst I was getting a twist of whelks down me in Bideford in 1784.

Did you know, Dear Hearts, that a curious anomaly of going back in time just long enough to eat a portion of whelks and then popping back to your own time is that the whelks stay where they are, whilst you move? A curious sensation, I must say, but it does mean that I get all the benefit of eating the things without having to worry about the calories. I'm just hunting out the best era for cream cakes now, don't you know?

Anyway, I'm meandering again. What was I saying? Oh yes, I was very surprised to see Smuckle in that part of the world and was just about to say hello when he tried to shoot me. With a gun, if you please.

Well, I was quick on the uptake and thought myself out of there somewhat sharpish. Of course, he was still in his original time and hadn't been tamed yet. Anyway, when I got back to the present I went straight to the lounge bar in *The Duke* to have a word with him.

"Why didn't you tell me we'd had another encounter?" I said.

"I was embarrassed," was his rather weak reply.

"Have we had any more?"

"Well, one or two – that's why I was so surprised when you saved me."

To be honest, he did look a bit bashful. He seemed to be struggling with something and a thought popped into my head.

"Oh well, I suppose I'd better not ask about the others. Except, do you kill me?"

"Probably not," was his somewhat evasive reply.

Best not to ask too directly, so I let it drop. One thing I did want to ask, though, was how he had escaped from drowning when he'd thrown himself overboard into the sea from the Revenue corvette, bound in heavy, iron chains, back in the last book.

"Well, all I knew was that I was knocked out when I hit the water and I was rather surprised to wake up back in bed at the hideout on Lundy. Do you know, now that I'd seen it in the daylight, they'd gone and done the walls the wrong colour?"

If you haven't got a clue what he was talking about, Dear Hearts, then go and buy the first book immediately!

Anyway, he went on.

"I decided not to bother thinking about it. I mean, there was no way that I could have got all those chains off me and then swum home. But because I couldn't account for it, I decided to just accept it. It wasn't until I had a little chat with myself on The Ferry just after you'd rescued me that I started to think things through again."

So I'd been right. I had seen two Smuckles for a few moments.

"What exactly was it that you said to yourself?" I asked.

Smuckle looked a bit sheepish again.

"Well, I said that if I fell in with you and the Captain instead of killing you, like I'd promised myself I'd do, you'd see me rich beyond my wildest dreams for the rest of my life. Sorry, it was the best incentive I could think of for myself at the time."

Yes, I could see him listening to that and going for the main chance. As to his escape from drowning, he went on.

"Well, I realised as soon as I arrived in your time that someone must have intervened to save me because I was unconscious and powerless to save myself. So I'm planning to go forward in time to where the relevant technology exists to hire a mini-sub and then take it back in time to save myself."

"What, you haven't done it yet?" I replied, somewhat shocked. "Isn't that leaving things to chance a bit?"

"Not a bit of it; plenty of time yet. Money to make and all that first," he said, rubbing his hands together and grinning like a maniac, consequently showing some very dodgy dental fretwork. Well, Smuckle may have moved into the present day, but his teeth remained somewhat endearingly in the eighteenth century.

Still, as to his attitude to the old folding dinero, I drank to that one and turned back to the *Financial Times* to see how my Pill Brewery shares were doing. Ah, very well indeed. Which called for a drink.

And this, complete with Milk Stout in paw, seems to be as good a place as any to end this particular set of reminiscences. So goodbye, Dear Hearts, do be good and I'll see you again one of these days.

10. Coda

Did I just say above that that was a good place to finish? Well, perhaps there's just a little something that I should mention before I sign off. And do please keep this a secret between ourselves, Dear Hearts, because I haven't told anyone else yet.

It's to do with my knitting bag. You'll remember that I checked it thoroughly to make sure that there was nothing missing before I escaped from *The Black Spot*. Well, there was just one tiny thing that I overlooked; although there was nothing missing from my knitting bag, there was something in it that had not been there before and which I didn't notice until long after I was reunited with it back here in Pill.

When the Eternal Doorman took the bag from me I couldn't help but notice that he wore a very singular ring. Yes, Dear Hearts, somehow that ring ended up in a dark corner of my knitting bag. I know now that what he said when we left *The Black Spot* was right. I'll be back there one day. I have to give him his ring back with my own paws. It's another of The Rules.

The bare bones of nameless dread have now been clothed with words that give name and shape, and thus full horror, to that dread. I now know, clearly and starkly, what only gnawed at the dark recesses of my unconscious before. What I am afraid of, Dear Hearts, when it comes down to it, is the inevitable; I'm afraid of Last Orders.

So it looks as though he won after all, Dear Hearts. I shouldn't think that I'll escape *The Black Spot* a second time. Last Orders will come for me one day, as inevitably as one Milk Stout follows another. But not yet awhile, Dear Hearts, not yet. Certainly not until The-One-That-Runs-It-All gets a proper database administrator.

Let's all drink to that; warm milk, of course, in your cases, my little ones.

Further Adventures of Tabitha Miggins...

About the author

After the first book was published under the pleasantly-fluffy name of Philippa Perry it came to light that there was a rather more famous Philippa Perry out there with books to her name. Therefore, it had to be admitted that the Philippa Perry of Miggins fame didn't really exist; or, at least, she did, but she was a he – to whit one Mark Clinton Jones.

So why did Mark see the need for a name and sex change? Well, he already had a series of extremely well-received music-related books to his real name and didn't really want to get people all confused by adding a half-witted set of childish adventures to the mix. So he chose Phil Perry because it was (phonetically, at least) a Spoonerism of Pill Ferry. That still didn't sound fluffy enough, so Phil became Philippa. Yes, very fluffy indeed; that'll do. But now it's back to the real name; so we have to unfluff with a vengeance.

Mark Clinton Jones was born in December, 1962, on the day that what became known as the Big Freeze of 1963 began. When the snow had cleared enough for the ambulance to get through he took up residence in Shirehampton, Bristol, where he continued to live, on and off, until the mid-1990s. In the early years, he often used the Pill Ferry and was rather sad when the service was discontinued in 1974. What has always surprised him is that, in Pill, the Ferry was officially (and somewhat logically, when you think about it) called 'The Shirehampton Ferry'. Luckily, though, this is not the version that has passed into song and from there into local folklore.

In 1996, fed up with the low pay, drudgery and all-embracing feeling of underachievement that went with working in a series of menial posts in the NHS and one or two private hospitals*, Mark eventually enrolled at university and got those qualifications he'd always promised himself. Quite good ones too – certainly good enough to decide on a career in higher education, though the fact is that he'd already started teaching before he'd even got as far as his second year (oh those lucky souls in the Engineering Faculty). He's always claimed that the experience he gained whilst teaching is what provided him with the necessary arrogance to go on and start writing. There again, he'd say anything, he's that arrogant.

On the surreal side, since the last Miggins book, Mark was rather surprised to be nominated for an international, academic award for research excellence for one of his 'serious' books. He has also started a series of database development and design books and claims that these are almost as much fun to write as Miggins because, as he says, writing about databases includes a great deal of creative fiction, such as, "...you'll find normalisation very easy to pick up," or, "...you can then simply implement your data model using any popular end-user relational database software." It's criminal, really!

So, all appears to be rosy, but on the downside *Tabitha Miggins, the Ballad Opera* has so far not become a reality, though he has received a few funny looks whenever mentioning the idea, which is often, and neither does Aardman seem to be close to offering a seriously large figure to turn the first book into its next animated blockbuster. Still, it's only a matter of time. And there's lots of that stuff about. Miggins certainly has an abundance of it.

Oh yes, whilst I think of it, just don't talk to me about pictures; I haven't even bothered to start thinking about them yet. And I've already spent the fee, so where's my incentive, eh?

Birdie (1, Railway Cottages, Pendomer, nr. East Coker, November 2015)

*He may one day write a book about what really goes on – you'll never want to go to hospital again, especially not a private one.

Further Adventures of Tabitha Miggins...

What others are saying about Miggins

Yet another magnificent book...I mean, what can I say? The new book...has it all. Panache, style, a good plot, well written...
The Tickenham Tatler

Here we go again; the author should have worked out by now that bunging together a set of old and pointlessly overworked jokes and interspersing them with a few bits of plot just isn't enough to keep the attention wandering to contemplation of more pleasurable activities, such as re-pointing your external walls – and don't forget that lime, sand and white cement are all on offer this month.
Wraxall & District Builders' Supplies Monthly Newsletter

Kate Hardcastle may have stooped to conquer, but Tabitha Miggins stoops to centrifuge...
Denny Island Advertiser

Well, it's all jolly good fun, and I must say that I'm surprised at Tabitha being so 'progressive'. I mean, starting a book at Chapter 2. How amusing!
Lavinia, CIO, Dream Cheese PLC

What does "mysql> DROP DATABASE all_heavens_master_db;" do I wonder? Well, that all looks a lot tidier, I must say.
Lavinia's Kevin (Note: the Over-Heaven Database Administrator post is currently vacant)

Yet another magnificent book from the same author that brought you *Calico Joe* and *Sycamore Row*. I mean, what can I say? The new book, *Rogue Lawyer*, has it all. Panache, style, a good plot, well written and...oh, hang on, I've got the wrong book haven't I? Oh, the Miggins one? Well, scrub everything I've just said for a start and all I'll say is... [ed: not quite sure where he picks up this sort of language – probably best not to publish it... and, whilst I'm at it, are you sure that you meant to include this?].
The Tickenham Tatler

Further Adventures of Tabitha Miggins...

Legalise calypso cigarettes now!
Natty Dreadcat, Inner Babylon Herald

We all laughed a great deal over the bit about Kevin losing access to his own back-end. After all, although we don't get out much and tend not to get asked to parties, we still know a funny joke about databases when the cleaner points it out to us. However, that aside, I don't think that the author really understands the many and varied (and not to say subtle) ways in which database administrators can keep track of macros and other embedded commands within a mysql database. However, before we can provide an authoritative answer to that, we need to know whether the author is referring to single, standalone macros or to macro groups, because there will be differences in the way in which searches can be performed against both. This is important because the term 'macro' is often used to refer to singular macro objects, but the author must understand that a given macro object can actually contain *multiple* macros. So, in a nutshell, these 'macro groups' are still displayed as a single macro object, but in reality will contain more than one macro. Of course, it is possible to create each single macro as a separate macro object, but it will generally save effort later on to group two or more related macros into a single macro object. Of course, this should all go without saying, but it's amazing how many miss this startlingly obvious fact. But to take a step back, I'm sure that most of your readers will understand that a single macro consists of individual macro actions, but that most actions will each require one or more arguments – and let's not forget, of course, that you can add conditions in the background to control how each action is run. Now, we'll just need to clarify these very obvious statements by looking at what is really going on in the background in terms of what is happening at machine code level when a macro is run from, say a remotely hosted server – and to clarify things, what I mean here when I say 'macro' is a *macro object* consisting, for the sake of argument, of multiple macros, all with numerous arguments and conditions, some of which are conditional on multiple other macro objects, themselves consisting of multiple...[next 40 pages removed for the sake of sanity].
Database Administration News Monthly

Further Adventures of Tabitha Miggins...

If it was us, we'd stick to the knitting and certainly not even think about faking any data or anything. Anyway, that was all a mistake – Peters never did say that. No, what he said was that he'd once dated a faker; a funny thing to say, I always thought, but that was after one of his hokey-cokey cigarettes, so what do you expect? Anyway, back to the point – yes, Brindle Holm does exist. How do we know? We asked Xerox. We would have asked Atari too, but they didn't answer the phone.

Peters & Waterman (authors of 'In Search of Brindle Holm')